Alpines in the Open Garden

The Rock Gardener's Library also includes:

Jack Elliott

Alpines in the Open Garden

CHRISTOPHER HELM
A & C BLACK · London

TIMBER PRESS
Portland, Oregon

Line illustrations by Duncan Lowe

First published 1991 by Christopher Helm (Publishers) Ltd,
a subsidiary of A & C Black (Publishers) Ltd,
35 Bedford Row, London WC1R 4JH

ISBN 0–7136–8100–4

A CIP catalogue record for this book is available from the British
Library

First Published in North America in 1991 by
Timber Press, Inc.
9999 SW Wilshire
Portland, Oregon 97225
USA

ISBN 0–88192–200–5

Typeset by Paston Press, Loddon, Norfolk
Printed and bound in Great Britain by Biddles, Ltd, Guildford, Surrey

Contents

Colour Plates

1. *Celmisia asteliifolia* (sun-loving/mid-season)
2. *Geranium* 'Lawrence Flatman' (sun-loving/mid-season)
3. *Sisyrinchium macounii album* (sun-loving/mid-season)
4. Rock garden with *Hypericum olympicum* and *Moltkia intermedia* (sun-loving/mid-season)
5. *Lithodora diffusa* 'Heavenly Blue' and *Penstemon scouleri albus* (sun-loving/mid-season)
6. *Roscoea cautleoides* (sun-loving/mid-season)
7. *Campanula haylodgensis* 'Warley White' (sun-loving/mid-season)
8. *Mertensia maritima* (sun-loving/mid-season)
9. *Linum salsoloides* 'Nanum' (sun-loving/mid-season)
10. *Aquilegia flabellata* (sun-loving/mid-season)
11. *Zauschneria* 'Glasnevin' (sun-loving/late-season)
12. *Cyclamen hederifolium* (shade-loving/late season)
13. *Ranunculus ficaria* 'Brazen Hussy' (shade-loving/early season)
14. *Glaucidium palmatum* and *Phylliopsis hillieri* 'Pinocchio' (shade-loving/early season)
15. *Corydalis ambigua* (shade-loving/early season)
16. *Dicentra eximia* and 'Luxuriant' (shade-loving/mid-season)
17. *Phlox adsurgens* (shade-loving/early season)
18. *Rhododendron camschaticum* (shade-loving/early season)
19. *Primula vialii* (shade-loving/mid-season)
20. *Erythronium oregonum, Sanguinaria canadensis* 'Plena' and *Camellia* (shade-loving/early season)

Illustrations

1 Introduction to My Garden

I have been an enthusiastic grower of alpine plants ever since the age of fifteen, when I first discovered a book illustrated with their colour photographs. That started a love-affair which has never dwindled – in fact, it was only after moving to a larger garden of tremendous potential seventeen years ago, that I started growing other plants with anything like the same keenness.

In spite of my own life-long enthusiasm for them, I am very much aware that alpines have a bad image among gardeners in general, an image which I hope to improve in this book. 'They are all very difficult', 'You have to have a rock garden for them', 'Aren't they the same as cacti?' are some favourite responses to any admission of interest in alpines. There is even some dichotomy among the societies specialising in them: the Alpine Garden Society and the New Zealand Alpine Garden Society firmly grasping the nomenclatural nettle, but the Scottish Rock Garden Club, and the American Rock Garden Society, together with the Royal Horticultural Society's Joint Rock Garden Plant Committee, perhaps feeling that 'rock garden plants' are more appealingly down-to-earth than 'alpines'.

'Rock plants' suggests that all alpines need a rock garden – an illusion which I would like to dispel immediately. 'Alpines' is a short easy term, to which I shall adhere, but I would like to define alpines as broadly as possible as being any small hardy perennials. Having given myself the maximum scope, what sort of plants are covered by this delightfully vague definition?

For the gardener of catholic tastes there are the high alpines from all the world's mountains, the small hardy woodlanders of Europe, the United States, the Himalayas, Japan and elsewhere, hardy bulbs and other Mediterranean plants, plants from the high plateaux of the United States, Turkey and China – in fact, any plants that might be hardy in a British garden, and are small enough to conform to one's own ideas of 'alpineness'. The Royal Horticultural Society defines 'rock garden plants' very reasonably as plants *suitable* for the rock garden. Look at the rock gardens at Wisley or at Kew, with their use of massive rocks, and you may see plants 3 ft (1 m) high or more, looking perfectly at home. This broadens the range too much and 12 in (30 cm) high is perhaps a more satisfactory limit in general. I say in general, because the enthusiast is likely to stretch a point to embrace such beauties as *Meconopsis* and *Nomocharis*, with the justification that they grow at 'alpine' altitudes and in 'alpine company' in the wild.

1

But are they difficult? 'Alpines are easy' is my main message in this book, but at the same time I know that many gardeners relish a challenge, and in no department of horticulture is there more scope to satisfy this particular whim than in alpine growing, as witnessed by the amazingly fine specimens of challenging plants to be seen at shows held by the Alpine Garden Society or Scottish Rock Garden Club. Many of these plants need immense skill and dedication and day-by-day attention, but many also are grown in pots purely for exhibition and, in fact, would grow even better in the open garden. Many alpine plants are too easy to appeal to exhibitors or judges but are wonderful garden plants, whether grown together on a rock garden or in a special bed, or in association with other larger plants. These are the plants I want to describe in this book, with a few brief words at the end to encourage those whose appetites have been whetted on easy plants and would like to try more challenging alpines.

Alpines can be used in many ways, of which the classical rock garden is the most difficult to do well. In the first garden which I made in Kent I built a rock garden with the local Kentish ragstone. Looking back on it, 'rock garden' was a euphemism for a series of raised beds, built into the slight natural slope – the easiest way to deal with any sloping site. Seventeen years ago we moved to our present garden, a perfectly flat site with several stone walls, and here I made two raised beds of moderate size, raised only by one course of ragstone walling stone, but with plenty of peat and grit incorporated into the soil. No-one would call these beds rock gardens, but they are the only beds devoted purely to alpines and dwarf bulbs; they have a backing of a wall on one side and a trellis on the other, both generously planted with assorted climbers to give a tall backdrop.

Elsewhere in the garden there are abundant alpines but they are associated with larger plants. In front of the walls I have made raised beds, usually at least two courses of rock high, to give planting crevices – wonderful sites for planting alpines. Where these beds are sunny I have made use of the sheltered positions to grow larger plants of borderline hardiness, between the alpines in front and the climbers or wall shrubs behind. The north-facing beds have been built up with rock in the same way, but the compost is made up largely of peat and leaf-mould. Here shade-loving alpines are associated with such woodland bulbs as erythroniums and trilliums, with extra height provided by ericaceous shrubs, including camellias and the more tender rhododendrons.

In the main part of the garden away from the walls, there are a number of borders. In some of these shrubs predominate, but I have tried to interplant them with the sort of easy ground-covering alpines that I shall describe later, for want of a better term, as 'easy carpeters'. In the earliest days I had one bed largely devoted to old-fashioned roses, and I grew various dianthus species and hybrids as a foreground to them. These flowered at the same time as the roses and matched their colours, giving a sumptuous pink and white effect from ground level upwards during June and July. This bed was in a very sheltered

2

part of the garden and I eventually moved the roses elsewhere and planted it with a mixture of tender plants and alpines.

In another bed with modern and species roses I have chosen alpines which will prolong the flowering period, rather than give an even greater impact during the rose season. There are drifts of dwarf narcissi flowering early, followed by groups of yellow doronicums and of varieties of *Primula denticulata* in blue, pink and white, followed again by some of the shade-loving phlox species such as *P. divaricata* and *P. stolonifera* in blue and pink. As these go over, later colour is provided by geraniums, the white *G. sanguineum* var. *album*, the blue 'Buxton's Blue' and several others, and by forms of *Viola cornuta*.

In some borders herbaceous plants predominate, with a background of tall shrubs, grasses and clematis. Here I have used alpines to bring the colour down to ground level, especially in two borders which are devoted to later-flowering perennials in pastel shades. Low-growing dianthus, campanulas, diascias and violas make a tremendous contribution to the overall scheme, which is at its best from July to September. It would have been just as easy to make the front of the borders early-flowering and the back late. This is a personal choice between having the longest possible flowering period and having the maximum impact for two or three months. I have tried to enjoy the best of both worlds by having these two colourful late summer borders in pastel shades, and most of the rest of the garden a mixed medley of plants, but always with alpines playing an important part.

The small size of alpines means you can grow a vast number of different plants in a small area. I find that all my enthusiastic gardening friends complain constantly that their gardens are full, and even with a couple of acres I have the same problem! Every winter the lawn shrinks a little or I 're-do' areas which have become filled with a neglected tangle of large shrubs and perennials, in order to accommodate new treasures. I choose more and more small plants, so that I can grow perhaps a dozen where one large shrub grew before, and – dare I say it? – I probably get twelve times the pleasure. On the other hand there is a tendency for modern gardens to be smaller and smaller, and the interest of a small garden is largely dependent upon the number of plants it contains. The alpine enthusiast may well be able to grow a thousand or more plants in a garden which would support less than a quarter of this number of shrubs or even larger perennials, and yet with this *multum in parvo* it will still be possible to have the contrast of height, shape and colour which is so important in creative gardening.

Unless I am using plants which I know enjoy heavy soil, I usually take the simple step of digging as much grit as I can spare into the areas in which I am going to plant alpines in mixed borders. It is worth bearing in mind that incorporating extra drainage will do no harm whatsoever to the large plants with which you are going to associate the alpines; indeed it will be of special benefit to any that are of doubtful hardiness. I shall discuss the importance of soil conditions in more detail at the end of this chapter.

3

For the smallest and (to me!) most exciting plants, a rock garden or a specially prepared bed will provide optimum conditions. The design and building of any rockwork is important (this will also be discussed in Chapter 4 devoted to practical matters). I must stress the importance of the plants themselves, especially on a flat site or simple raised bed, when the flatness can be relieved by the careful siting of larger plants and shrubs, for example dwarf conifers. It is easy to look upon such a bed as a home for a collection of alpine plants, without giving any thought to the overall picture. I think many gardeners – and I must include myself – take some pains to plan their herbaceous or mixed borders with an eye to colour, flowering season and variation in form, and yet when it comes to planting alpines in a bed of their own are content with a complete hotchpotch. In practice, this works quite adequately because the plants are all attractive and rarely scream at each other! On the other hand, such a bed could be made to look much more attractive, and fit much better into the whole garden context, if similar thought is given to its planning. Variations in height and growth habit, and subtle colour combinations of plants flowering together, can greatly improve the overall effect.

I mentioned earlier the shady raised beds in my garden, which are one of the most interesting features during spring and early summer. I feel that, far from being the problem that gardeners seem to consider it, shade adds another welcome dimension to gardening. If fate bequeathed that I should have nothing but shade or nothing but sun in my garden, I sometimes think that I would choose the former, because so many shade-loving alpines seem to me to have a special delicacy and beauty lacking in the more spectacular sun-lovers. The shady areas of the garden can be just as interesting and colourful as those in sun, but the whole effect is likely to be more restrained. Having said that, a word of warning is necessary! Do not hack out a square foot or two of roots under dense deciduous cover, and expect to grow shortias or meconopsis! The ideal shade bed is an area free from roots, perhaps in the shade of a wall, or to the north of tall trees and at a reasonable distance from them. Bear in mind just how high the sun is at midsummer, or some of your shade-lovers may be roasted, as happens along the edge of one of my peat beds, shaded by a not very high wall. Your soil in the shade will almost certainly need improving – these plants are great humus-lovers – and as much peat and leaf-mould as possible should be dug into the top spit of any shade bed, preferably with well-rotted manure underneath. For the alpine grower the most exciting development of shade gardening is the peat garden, in which raised beds are made with peat blocks instead of stone walls, and the soil is composed to a very large extent of peat. This will be described in more detail in Chapter 4.

There are several special situations in which alpines can be invaluable. Many gardeners have retaining walls, for example where the drive or paths have been cut out of a slope, and these can be made into colourful features. There is a good range of suitable plants for them, many of which actually prefer to be planted on their sides, whether in sun or shade. It is of course vital that the soil behind the wall is suitably prepared as there is probably only subsoil behind the lower courses, or even builders' rubble.

Alpines look marvellous in containers, especially in old sinks and troughs, which are now very scarce; however, good imitations can be made from 'hypertufa' (see p. 124). Containers of this sort can be filled with the ideal compost for the particular plants, and some of the more difficult alpines thrive in them. Growing alpines in pots will be discussed briefly in Chapter 4, as will the use of tufa, a strange rock which is light and porous and can easily be drilled to take plants, many of which seem to grow better in it than in any other way.

Growing Conditions

Long and loud though we moan about our climate, a wider range of plants can be grown successfully in the British Isles than anywhere else on earth, and our broadly defined 'alpines' are probably the largest group of garden plants. Considering the remarkable range of habitats in which alpines naturally grow, it is not surprising that even here the nature of the basic soil, the rainfall in summer and winter, the extremes of temperature, all have an effect on what plants we can grow, as does the direction of any slope and the presence or absence of shade. Although these are mainly factors over which we have no control, their effects can be modified to a greater or lesser extent.

Some areas, and indeed some gardens, grow certain plants much better than others. Friends in Scotland sometimes tell me that they cannot grow bulbs, a generalisation that I take with a pinch of salt, and counter with the equally dogmatic statement that 'I cannot' or, more dangerously, 'You cannot grow Asiatic primulas in Kent'! Maybe my northern friends should stick to growing Asiatic primulas like cabbages among their swathes of ericaceous shrubs, and I should concentrate on bulbs and plants for hot dry areas, and we should revel in our successes. However, gardeners are not like that, so we do everything possible to modify our climatic and geographical factors. I dig in lots of peat, leaf-mould and well-rotted manure, and water all through May and June while our dry east wind howls across the garden, in order to grow primulas and meconopsis which I know will be mere shadows of what they can be in the north, while my northern friends make south-facing screes for the ardent sun-lovers, which may well still look as if they are pining for warmer climes.

Some plants are admittedly exacting in their requirements, but most are surprisingly adaptable, which is why you can grow Turkish bulbs through a carpet of raoulias from the damp mountain tops of New Zealand, beneath shrubs from the Nevada desert.

Although I shall suggest ways of modifying the more difficult soils and conditions to enable as many plants as possible to be grown, and indicate sun and shade requirements, it is worth remembering the oft-quoted maxim that if you have three plants of a species, plant one where you think it will grow, one where others tell you it will grow, and one where nobody thinks it will grow.

Gardening is full of surprises and often the third site will be the most successful. Plants seeding themselves around will often give you a hint by putting themselves in the 'wrong' place and thriving there, notably in shade when they should prefer full sun, or vice versa. In no other field is there such scope for experiment, and for confounding the expert, whose expertise is sometimes based on untried hearsay.

Having said the plants will often adapt to your conditions, I must tell you that if these conditions are particularly bad for alpines, some improvements will be needed to make them congenial to particular plants. Unfortunately, the pH content is important and (dare I say it?) unchangeable if you have a strongly alkaline soil. Various suggestions are sometimes made to enable gardeners on limy or chalky soils to grow lime-hating plants. The best solution is to grow them only in containers and, if possible, water them with rain water. Beds raised well above the surrounding soil and incorporating as much peat as possible, may work for a year or two, especially with a polythene sheet beneath them, to prevent the lime creeping in from below. Eventually, however, the plants will begin to suffer, although watering with Sequestrene may help to keep them going for a while. The best advice for those who garden on such a soil is to enjoy all the plants that actually prefer a high pH, such as dianthus and saxifrages, advice that is likely to be spurned by those determined to grow Asiatic gentians or Ericaceae!

Extremes of acidity are much less worrying as they can be modified by adding lime, but if your pH is around 6.0, rejoice in the fact that few, if any, plants actually suffer from slight acidity, and remember you cannot take the lime away again.

Heavy soils are the least suitable for growing alpines, and a really sticky clay is going to need hard work! On the other hand, if you can modify them, clay soils will then grow many plants better than the sandy soils which need constant feeding. A famous alpine grower of the past, Captain Mooney, gardened on heavy Wealden clay in Kent and grew a remarkable range of alpine plants, many of them considered difficult, like the beautiful *Pulsatilla alpina* of the Alps. The secret of his success was an eight-inch layer of pure shingle on top of the soil, into which the alpines were planted. This surfacing gave rapid drainage to carry water away from the collars of the plants, always the danger area in heavy soils, while their roots found their way to the very nourishing clay beneath. If your soil is more or less undiggable this is the simplest solution, but the layer of grit must be deep. The grit should be very coarse, shingle or granite chippings, or other material with a diameter up to half an inch (1.3 cm) If you have a soil that is heavy but diggable, there may be a few small perennials that will grow for you, but digging in plenty of coarse grit – mine is from 3/16ths of an inch (0.3 cm) down to sand – will make all the difference to the range available to you.

The opposite extreme to a heavy clay soil is a light sandy soil, which you can dig even on the wettest of winter days – a great joy, but again there is a snag, in that the soil lacks nutrient and dries out rapidly. My previous garden had just

Figure 1   Pulsatilla alpina

such soil, which looked like the Bagshot Sand on which Wisley and many of the Surrey and Hampshire nurseries stand. This soil was a joy to work with, but it needed the incorporation of masses of peat and leaf-mould, and when possible farmyard manure. However, manure needs to be treated with care, as many alpines and especially ericaceous shrubs, which love such a light soil, dislike manure unless it is very old. If you have a source, put it under the top spit, then dig leaf-mould and peat into the higher levels.

Rainfall is an important factor, which is interactive with the amount of shade and the summer temperature range. One cannot be too dogmatic about this, because a plant which flourishes in full sun in the North, especially in a high summer rainfall area, may well need a shady position in the South, unless it is heavily watered during summer. Conversely, the many plants accustomed to a dry summer in their natural haunts, will flourish in the South-Eastern counties with a rainfall of around 20 in (50 cm), falling mainly in winter, but will only grow under glass or in exceptionally well-drained positions in the North or wetter areas of the West. Many of the most beautiful alpines come from the Himalayas and from the mountains of New Zealand where the humidity is very high even in summer. It is difficult to emulate these conditions in a garden with low rainfall, as I have found to my cost in Kent, but incorporating as much humus as possible, providing shade, and watering during dry spells, gives you the best possible chance of success.

To summarise, alpines generally enjoy a well-drained soil with plenty of humus and adequate moisture. This should be the aim, and to achieve it gardeners with very sandy soil, or with hot dry gardens, will need to add humus and will probably still have to water in summer, and gardeners in areas of heavy rainfall or with heavy soils will have to incorporate extra drainage material. Further practical details will be given in Chapter 4.

2 Sun-loving Alpines

In considering alpines to grow in a sunny garden I propose to group them according to their season of flowering, and further sub-divide them into easy carpeting plants, typical clump-forming alpines, and shrubs. Among the 'easy carpeters' I have included other robust, undemanding plants that are excellent as a foreground to larger plants but may be too rampant for the rock garden or raised bed. To have an impact in a mixed border the more typical alpines need to be planted in groups, but they will hold their own when associated with other plants of similar size. Alpine shrubs vary enormously in height from diminutive species of an inch or two, to spreading bushes of a foot or more, and their use varies accordingly.

Early Season

No description of early-flowering alpines would be complete without some mention of bulbous plants, as these provide the major part of the garden display until early April, and continue to contribute until the end of the month.

In my own garden the first hopeful sign of spring comes as early as January, given a few mild spells, with the flowering of the deep blue *Iris histrioides* 'Major', followed within a week or two by its hybrid 'Katherine Hodgkin', an easy and rapidly increasing bulb with flowers in an intriguing mixture of blue, green and yellow, not liked by everyone but very welcome at that time of year. Everything depends on the weather but, in addition to the blue of *I. histrioides* 'Major' followed by the other Reticulata irises, I like to plant some early narcissi for contrasting winter colour, for example *Narcissus romieuxii* or *N.* 'Nylon', which flower from December onwards and withstand the weather amazingly well. At the same time the earliest of my crocuses commence flowering, usually *Crocus imperati*, which has purple flowers with the outside of the petals feathered with deep maroon.

As the weather improves in February the number of flowering bulbs increases dramatically, with yellow carpets of dwarf narcissi such as *N. bulbocodium* and its varieties, the blue of the later Reticulata irises, and chionodoxas and scillas which, I find, sow themselves around to provide masses of colour, contrasting marvellously with the narcissi even in the wilder parts of the garden. The crocuses also can be planted en masse or left to build up into worthwhile patches of white, yellow or lavender blue. Later still the smaller tulip species and fritillaries make ideal associates for the alpine plants which, by then, are beginning to flower on the rock garden.

Easy Carpeters

The trio of aubretia, alyssum and arabis, maybe with the addition of iberis, are the archetypal colour carpets seen in half the gardens of Britain in spring. They are intensely colourful for a week or two, trouble-free until their size and age become problems, and unbeatable when grown in or at the top of a retaining wall, where they form waterfalls of colour in what might be considered a difficult situation. Having said that, they are not for the alpine enthusiast in any other situation as their very success as ground-cover means that they take up too much space that might be used for more exciting plants. Also, the foliage after flowering is a mess in the case of aubretia and without much merit in any of the others. Cut these plants back after the flowers fade.

The best aubretias in general cultivation are all hybrids, and should be grown as named cultivars rather than seedlings, as these are far superior. Any catalogue will list several in a range of colours which includes pale to dark blue, and pale pink through to darkish purple. They are easily propagated from cuttings. If you like variegated plants, there are also one or two varieties with good variegated leaves and deep blue flowers, which I think are worth growing in a choicer situation.

For a yellow carpet the popular alyssums are cultivars of *Alyssum saxatile*, the species itself or its more compact variety 'Compactum' with bright yellow flowers, the subspecies *citrinum* with pleasant pale yellow flowers, and 'Dudley Neville' with buff-coloured flowers (which also has a good variegated form that is not excessively vigorous). In addition to these, the genus includes some more compact and dainty species often with silvery leaves.

Arabis is a large genus, not all of which can be called easy carpeters, and these are mainly clones of *A. caucasica*. The double-flowered 'Plena' is one of the best of these for a white carpet, and there are several named pink varieties. *A. ferdinandi-coburgi* also has white flowers and is usually grown in its more useful variegated leaf forms, with either white or yellow variegation. *A. blepharophylla* can hardly be classed as an easy carpeter but is an excellent deep rose-coloured species needing a well-drained site.

Iberis sempervirens makes a steadily-widening mat of reasonably attractive evergreen rosettes with masses of pure white flowers in spring, but it needs plenty of room eventually, and I am not sure that it is worth the space! There are one or two other named cultivars, but all are white.

Having dealt with the ultra-vigorous carpeters so good for growing on retaining walls, I can now describe some more appealing (to me?) genera of similar but less vigorous habit. First and foremost among these I would pick the sun-loving phlox, mainly cultivars and hybrids of *Phlox subulata* and *P. douglasii*, in a range of colours including white, pale to deepest lavender to purple, and from pale pink to deepest magenta. Many others will be considered under alpines for shade, as this beautiful genus has plants for every situation, including some to tax the skill of the enthusiast.

Nomenclature is a problem here and some of the varieties will be found under *P. douglasii* in one catalogue and under *P. subulata* in another. Therefore, unless nurseries have decided to list them all alphabetically, it is worth trying under both headings if you are searching for a particular plant. On the whole the varieties of *P. douglasii* are more compact, and their needle-like leaves smaller than those of *P. subulata*, which will probably spread a little further and faster.

Single plants of any one variety of phlox will spread sufficiently widely to make a splash of colour, but if you have the space then groups of three look even better, as is true of most plants. The varieties can be mixed, but fair-sized drifts of each colour give the best effect. I like to use them singly in the rock garden, or in groups along the sunny side of borders, with larger shrubs and perennials, where they bring early colour a month or two before the main display begins. In heavy soil some extra drainage will be needed along this edge.

Any catalogue will list a considerable number of phlox and a choice can safely be made from these. Among my own favourites are the white 'May Snow', the old favourites among the lavender-blues, 'G.F. Wilson' and 'Boothman's Variety', and some of the modern pink to reddish shades, such as the vivid 'Crackerjack' (very neat and floriferous), 'Kelly's Eye' (pink with a dark centre) and the deep rose large-flowered 'McDaniel's Cushion', the last two particularly vigorous. The hottest colour of all is seen in another old hybrid, the brilliant magenta 'Temiscaming'.

One other carpeter deserves special mention as it is so easily grown and early-flowering (generally in March). This is *Doronicum cordatum* with large yellow daisies on 6 in (15 cm) stems. Although yellow is such a predominant colour in spring with forsythia above and daffodils below, the doronicum can make a striking contrast to scillas and chionodoxas. In a moist heavy soil less suitable for bulbs, I grow it to contrast with *Primula denticulata* and its varieties, which are in shades of lavender and pink.

The Major Alpine Genera

So many of the best alpine plants belong to a few important genera that I shall consider these first, concentrating on the easier species which will thrive in the open garden, but listing a few others whose beauty makes their special requirements worth the effort.

GENTIANS

Surely these are the most evocative of all! Anyone who has seen the sky-blue patches of *Gentiana verna* in the Alps or, on a more esoteric level, the drifts of autumn-flowering gentians in the Himalayas, will feel that these personify the best of alpines.

11

Figure 2   Gentiana acaulis

Much as we would all like to emulate in our gardens these amazing patches of blue, in the case of the spring gentians, *G. verna* or *G. verna* var. *angulosa*, this is not altogether easy. I find that I obtain the best results by growing them from seed, preferably sown in the autumn, which should germinate in spring. Against all general principles I do not prick the seedlings out separately but in small clumps. This minimises root disturbance and they seem to like each other's company. I like to pot up these clumps separately until they are large enough to plant out, but they can be planted straight outside in the garden. Plant them closer together than usual in a rich, gritty soil with abundant humus, and keep them well-watered. I find they do quite well in a raised bed for a year or two, especially with an annual top-dressing of leaf mould, but they never quite look the same as in the mountains!

The other spring-flowering gentian *G. acaulis* presents very different problems. It is easy to grow from seed or from young plants and will make a steadily increasing mat in any reasonably well-drained soil. If you are lucky your mat will be covered in spring with large deep-blue trumpets, but in some gardens it fails to flower. All sorts of suggestions have been made to overcome this, but most of them can be summarised in the advice to use very rich well-manured soil, to plant exceptionally firmly with the aid of a heavy boot, and, last but not least, to live well away from any pollution as this is thought to prevent flowering! Fortunately they flower well for me here in Kent!

In catalogues, various forms and allies of *G. acaulis* will be found. All are beautiful and, if they are successful, try as many as you can. *G. alpina* is

12

particularly neat and compact; the others vary slightly in colour and size of flower.

A few other spring-flowering species are found in specialist lists. These are mainly closer to *G. verna* and are even more difficult to satisfy, although they can sometimes be seen and admired at shows of the Alpine Garden Society – triumphs of alpine house cultivation. *Gentiana pyrenaica* and *G. pumila* are two of the most exciting, which can be tried outside in a raised scree bed. The remaining gentians will be described in the late season sections (see p. 64).

PRIMULAS

This is a genus of more than 500 species, all of which come within our definition of alpines and which contains a wealth of beautiful plants, from trouble-free garden plants to some of the most tricky alpine house species. The fact that any primula is worth growing makes their selection difficult, and although they have been split into thirty botanical sections, it is probably more helpful to the gardener if I divide them into groups with similar requirements and uses in cultivation, and select from these a personal choice of some of the best. There are always plenty more for the avid collector, and good literature in which to study them.

A geographical subdivision is surprisingly useful, as the Asiatic species, mainly from the Himalayas, generally require partial shade, moist conditions and a humus-rich soil, whereas the European species, with which I shall combine a few American species, mainly need full sun or only light shade and a more loamy soil, and will tolerate drier conditions. In view of these general requirements (and there are plenty of exceptions), I shall consider the European species here, except *Primula farinosa* and its allies, which have the same requirements as the Asiatics.

The primroses and polyanthus, in a vast number of varieties, are mainly of European origin and are so well-known and so readily available as plants or seed that they need not be considered here. Suffice it to say that they thrive in similar conditions enjoyed by the easier Asiatics and associate superbly with early-flowering shrubs and the taller narcissi and other bulbs. I enjoyed them for many years until birds started attacking the flowers. Then I became tired of cottoning them.

The auriculas are an important group of European primulas, but many of them, especially the show auriculas, are plants for the cold greenhouse that have a tremendous following among specialists. Although some of the 'alpine auriculas' can be grown outside, it is really the naturally occurring species and varieties and the so-called 'border auriculas' that do best in the garden, enjoying the well-drained conditions of a raised bed or rock garden. *Primula auricula* itself has yellow flowers with a white throat, and its beautiful subspecies *balbisii* is a smaller plant in all its parts, with deep yellow flowers. Even neater is the beautiful miniature *P. auricula* 'Blairside Yellow', which only attains an inch or two (2.5–5 cm) in height. The border auriculas are much larger and are of very long standing, and possibly are losing vigour. They include the velvety-blue 'Blue Velvet' and 'Old Irish Blue', the 'Old Red Dusty Miller' and 'Old Yellow Dusty Miller'. All these auriculas have the extra asset of good foliage, their large fleshy leaves often being dusted with white farina, especially under glass as this farina tends to be lost in wet weather.

I think the largest auriculas, especially the border varieties, are out of scale in the rock garden, particularly in the neighbourhood of small primulas. I prefer to grow them either as wall plants, where they are quite happy between rocks, or as an edging like the easy carpeters.

The name *Primula × pubescens* strictly speaking should be applied to hybrids between *P. auricula* and *P. latifolia*, but it seems to cover a range of more complex hybrids which are all invaluable plants for the rock garden. They make gradually increasing clumps of rosettes of leaves only 2–3 in (5–8 cm) high with flower stems up to 4 in (10 cm). As long as drainage is adequate they are easy to grow in a sunny position. The colour range is considerable. One of the finest is *P. × pubescens* 'Alba', not often offered nowadays, with globular heads of glorious large white flowers, but there are reasonable alternatives such as 'Bewerley White' or 'Harlow Car', in which the flowers are a more creamy-white. Some of my favourites from the considerable number available are 'Boothman's Variety', crimson with a white eye, 'Mrs J.H. Wilson', another good old hybrid with deep purple white-centred flowers, and 'Rufus', an unusual shade of brownish-red. For many years we enjoyed a robust hybrid under the name of *P. belluensis*, which now seems to be available as 'Freedom', an excellent plant with very deep lilac flowers. This is only a brief selection and any of those available can be recommended.

It is surprising how rarely we see *Primula marginata* planted in the open garden. This would come high in my list of favourite alpines, combining beautiful foliage at all times with very attractive flowers in the spring. It grows wild in the maritime alps, usually in fissures in the rock, and this gives a hint as to its cultivation. It is not difficult to grow in well-drained loamy soil, but my feeling is that it looks best and probably grows best planted on its side in a retaining wall, or at least between two rocks. The large rosettes of leaves are normally heavily farinose, especially along the beautifully toothed leaf margins, but some of this will be lost in wet conditions. Maybe that is why it is more often grown under glass, but the leaves are still beautiful in the open! The flowering stems are usually 3–4 in (8–10 cm) long and bear several flowers on each, generally from pale to deep lavender, although occasionally they are white with a tendency to washiness. Among the numerous varieties offered in catalogues all are good, but the largest flowers are seen on 'Linda Pope', which is probably a hybrid, with excellent heavily farinose leaves. I must admit that it looks even better in the alpine house! 'Beatrice Lascaris' is of very recent origin and has a particularly beautiful rosette of leaves. Study the catalogues for other varieties with deeper coloured flowers.

'Marven' is a very fine hybrid between *P. marginata* and the related *P. venusta*. The leaves are pale green dusted with farina and the flowers are deep

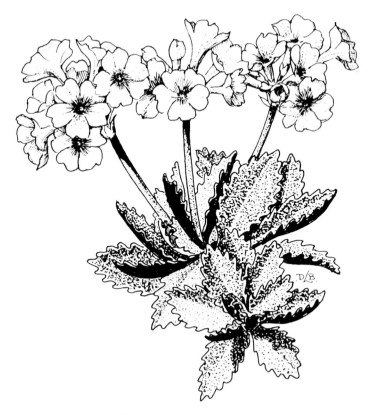

Figure 3   Primula marginata

violet with a darker eye, surrounded by a ring of white farina, as in many auriculas.

The species and hybrids so far listed probably include the easiest and most colourful of the European primulas, but we have hardly touched on the many species in cultivation. *P. latifolia*, a parent of *P. × pubescens*, is one of many rather similar species with rosettes of quite small leaves and short stems of one or more flowers in shades of reddish purple, pink or lavender. All of them will excite the primula enthusiast, but even he or she might admit that several are similar in appearance, and that some are difficult to grow or to flower satisfactorily. There is plenty of excellent literature to which the enthusiast can refer, but here I will confine myself to a few favourites which may encourage the grower to look further. Of all the species in this group I think *P. minima* and its white form are the most beautiful when they flower well: perhaps I should say 'would be', as usually I have to be content with only a flower or two. These flowers have very deeply notched petals carried on short stems above a rosette of dark green toothed leaves less than an inch high. The colour of the flowers is deep rose, or clear white in the albino variety.

Primula clusiana is typical of those species with rosettes of leathery deep green leaves with untoothed margins. The flower stems carry one to three deep-rose flowers above the leaves. It flowers more freely than *P. minima*, but for reliability in this respect the natural hybrid of *P. minima*, usually offered as *P.* × *bileckii* (strictly *P.* × *forsteri*), is outstanding as it is also more vigorous. *Primula carniolica* is a very distinct species, with rosettes of much longer glossy leaves and flower stems up to 8 in (20 cm) with as many as a dozen flowers on a stem in a one-sided umbel, the flowers deep rose with a farinose white eye.

These plants are all too small to associate with anything but alpines and small bulbs, and they do best in a rich scree mixture: that is, with plenty of humus and at least a third of its bulk of coarse grit.

There are several American primula species worth trying in the open garden in similar conditions of rich scree, or in a well-drained lightly shaded peat garden. None of them is common in cultivation and they are usually seen in pots in the alpine house, but I am growing them outside quite successfully. The most robust is *P. parryi* with 4 in (10 cm) long glossy pale green leaves and stems up to 6 in (15 cm) or more, with some white farina, bearing one-sided umbels of yellow-eyed deep rose to magenta flowers, the colour varying considerably. This description also fits *P. ellisiae*, which dies down completely in winter and commences growth in late spring. *P. rusbyi* is very similar, but smaller. One other species that is seen occasionally is *P. suffrutescens*, a curious plant of shrubby habit with a reputation for being difficult to grow, which I do not think is fully deserved. I grow it in a raised scree bed in full sun. It gradually forms woody stems with whorls of toothed leaves at the ends of, as well as along, the stems. The flowering stems arise from these rosettes and are usually 2–3 in (5–7 cm) long, with an umbel of deep rose yellow-eyed flowers.

SAXIFRAGA

This is an immense genus of similar or maybe greater complexity than *Primula* which, like that genus, has been subdivided into a considerable number of botanical groups. In a book that is mainly concerned with the garden use of alpine plants, it seems simplest again to ignore the botanical minutiae and divide the saxifrages according to their general appearance and their garden requirements. A broad division into sun-lovers and shade-lovers is a good start, as a major proportion of the species belongs either to the generally sun-loving encrusted or kabschia including engleria groups, or to the more shade-loving 'mossy' oppositifolia or fortunei groups, with a few odds and ends added to each! If these groups sound baffling already I shall try to clarify them individually, considering only the sun-lovers here.

The two main subdivisions differ markedly in their garden uses. The sun-lovers dealt with here are generally small plants for the rock garden, raised beds or retaining walls, whereas the shade-lovers are mainly easy and quite robust plants that can look after themselves even when associated with shrubs or larger perennials.

I used the terms kabschia and engleria as they were at one time separate botanical sections which made sense to gardeners, but they have now both been lumped into section Porophyllum (Kabschia). All these have attractive small rosettes, which are usually silver with lime encrustation, but in some species are green. They vary enormously in vigour, and can build up into a spreading mat of rosettes or into neat tight hummocks. In the kabschia group the flower stems may be very short with solitary flowers, or up to 2–3 in (5–7 cm) long with several flowers on a stem. In the englerias the rosettes tend to be larger and more lime-encrusted, often with a symmetry of form which is beautiful in itself, and their hairy flower stems are long, with reddish stem leaves and several flowers opening from deep pink to purple buds.

Although most of the englerias have reddish-purple stems and flowers, contrasting beautifully with the silver of the rosettes, the kabschia sections give us a fantastic range of colour, lacking only a true blue. They flower very early in the spring and are so floriferous that the leaves are often invisible at flowering time. For the rest of the year they have beautiful foliage which associates well with other small plants, making them ideal alpines which are attractive at all seasons. As the leaves of most species are silver, they can be used on the smallest scale in the same way as large silver foliage plants in the border, to soften or separate some of the harsher colours, or in combination, for example, with the reddish or purple leaves of some sedums and sempervivums. Most of these saxifrages are very small and require a very well-drained, preferably limy, soil with plenty of humus, so that the rock garden or raised bed suits them best. They make ideal trough plants or can be planted into lumps of tufa. In the southern counties I find they are sometimes scorched by hot sun, so they should be planted on a north slope, or in partial shade, but further north full exposure will suit them well. They also make superb alpine house plants where their early flowering can be enjoyed under cover. In a retaining wall with well-prepared soil behind it, the more robust kabschias will grow well planted on their side, filling the spaces between the rocks.

Numerous kabschia saxifrages are available from nurserymen, many of them hybrids raised during the 1930s and soon after the Second World War, when they enjoyed a great vogue. Like primulas, any of them are worth growing and I shall confine myself to a few reliable favourites.

Among the englerias the biggest and best is *Saxifraga grisebachii*, usually seen as its 'Wisley Variety'. This makes magnificent silver rosettes of perfect symmetry, with purple stems of flowers up to 4–5 in (10–12 cm) long. It can be grown in scree conditions or planted in tufa, but is better with some overhead protection; in fact, I would put it among the best dozen alpine house plants. A better open garden plant is *S. sempervivum*, possibly found under its old name as *S. porophylla*. In my garden this has done well in a raised bed, seeding itself around, especially into the tufa. It has smaller silver rosettes and much smaller

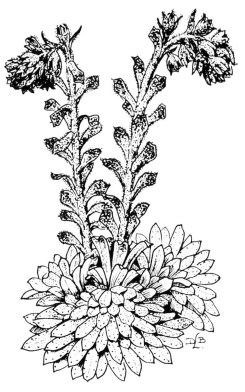

Figure 4   Saxifraga grisebachii

heads of deep purple flowers. Two other good englerias with beautiful rosettes, intermediate between the two mentioned in size and ease of cultivation, are *S. media* and the hybrid *S.* × *biasolettii* 'Crystalie', between *S. grisebachii* and *S. sempervivum*.

There are several beautiful pink to purple-flowered kabschias. Two of the easiest and most reliable are 'Cranbourne' and 'Jenkinsae', both pale pink. *S. megasaeflora* has exceptionally large, slightly frilled flowers, and 'Winifred' and 'Riverslea' both have much deeper-coloured flowers. Among the yellows, two of the most vigorous with green leaves are the pale *S. apiculata* and the deeper-coloured 'Elizabethae', both reliable rock garden plants. There are several with typical compact silver-grey cushions. Among the oldest is 'Faldonside' but this may be losing vigour, and a more modern hybrid such as 'Valerie Finnis' is a more reliable choice for the garden. The most vigorous white is probably *S. apiculata* 'Alba', but there is again a wide choice among those with more silver cushions. *S. burseriana* 'Gloria' or 'Major' have very large flowers, whereas *S. marginata* usually proves to be more vigorous with taller flowering stems. For plenty more choice consult the catalogues of specialist alpine growers.

The second major group of saxifrages for the sunny garden is the encrusted or silver group, botanically section Euaizoonia. These are magnificent plants which make a real impact in the garden, especially when used in walls. Typically they have large rosettes of heavily lime-encrusted leaves and abundant sprays of pure white flowers, but there is some colour variation and the rosettes can be less than one-third of an inch (1 cm) or more than 8 in (20 cm) across. Having said that alpine plants do not need rocks, I must confess to a preference for growing this group among, or preferably between, rocks, although the easier ones are perfectly happy planted on the flat.

The easiest of all is probably *S. aizoon* (*S. paniculata*), which has a wide range of different forms. The rosettes may be as little as a quarter of an inch (0.5 cm) across or more than one inch (2.5 cm) in the larger forms. The sprays of flowers are usually white, but in *S. aizoon* 'Lutea' they are pale creamy-yellow and in 'Rosea' pink. All of them have fine silvery-encrusted rosettes, usually with a more yellowish tinge than others in the section. In any well-drained site they will increase well, forming a mat of rosettes on the level or, better still, filling in the interstices between rocks. In my garden they thrive on tufa and seed freely into it until the rock is almost invisible.

S. cochlearis var. *minor* has tiny intensely silver rosettes, which will carpet the ground or cover tufa rocks. Like most of the section it flowers in May with short sprays of dainty white flowers. Among the many species with larger rosettes are *S. callosa* and *S. cotyledon*. These both have long narrow lime-encrusted leaves, forming rosettes up to 4 in (10 cm) across, but have several forms which differ in minor details. The handsome sprays of flowers are white, but in a few the petals may be dotted with pink. *S. cotyledon* is easy to grow, especially in partial shade, and makes a wonderful crevice plant with long sprays of small white flowers and fine rosettes pressed against the rock face.

The largest rosettes of all are produced by *S. longifolia*, especially when it is grown under glass. They can be 8 in (20 cm) across and each produces a stem up to 3 ft (1 m) long with thousands of flowers. This species looks wonderful growing out from a rock face, even when the flower stems in my own garden are only usually about 18 in (45 cm) long. After flowering, alas, the plant dies, but it can be grown from seed. The hybrid 'Tumbling Waters' closely resembles *S. longifolia*, but before flowering it produces several offsets that can be rooted and grown on. You can then plant several rosettes together to produce a wonderful waterfall effect, if they are in the crevices of a high enough retaining wall.

Two hybrids worth mentioning are 'Kathleen Pinsent' and 'Southside Seedling'. In the former the rosettes are very handsome and of medium size and the flowers are pale pink. 'Southside Seedling' is one of my favourite plants, especially for a rock crevice, with large rosettes like those of *S. cotyledon* but with flowers that are heavily spotted with red to give an overall impression of quite deep pink.

As wall plants all these silver saxifrages flower in early summer, so that they follow the rather coarse-leaved easy carpeters like aubretia, and can have the more refined company of the lewisias. The silver rosettes of the saxifrages are ornamental throughout the year and become a really striking feature during their flowering season.

RANUNCULUS

The buttercup genus contains some of our worst weeds and some of our most beautiful plants, from tiny alpines to large border plants. Almost all of them have the same exquisitely simple single flowers admired by wild flower lover and gardener alike, but the less the plants resemble native buttercups the more desirable they seem to be! The flowers can be the same or perhaps larger than the buttercup as long as the leaves are readily distinguishable and the plant is not invasive. Pick a flower from *Ranunculus gramineus* or *R. montanus* and you have an 'ordinary' buttercup, but the leaves and habit are so totally different that we happily admit them to the garden.

I mention these species as two of the easiest for the garden. *Ranunculus montanus* makes a slowly-spreading carpet of small, deep green leaves, from which arise short stems carrying solitary deep yellow flowers. It is usually seen as a very neat compact form, 'Molten Gold'. *Ranunculus gramineus* forms a clump of very narrow glaucous leaves, varying in height from 4–10 in (10–25 cm), overtopped by paler yellow flowers on slender stems. As long as the soil is not heavy they can be grown anywhere in a sunny spot, with other alpines or as a foreground to small shrubs.

Ranunculus ficaria, the lesser celandine, is probably a worse menace than many buttercups, but has several well-behaved varieties that will be considered with other shade-lovers and with the New Zealand buttercups. Most of the other small species require more specialised conditions with excellent drainage and lots of peat or leaf mould – rich scree in fact – so that they are usually grown on the rock garden or raised beds, the smallest species being ideal for troughs or in the alpine house.

Among the earliest flowering is *R. calandrinioides*, usually seen in the alpine house but quite possible to grow in scree. It has very attractive glaucous leaves, and stems up to 6 in (15 cm) with one to three large white flowers. These vary enormously but in the best forms are large and deeply flushed with pink. They often appear as early as February and are among the most beautiful of all alpines.

Later in the spring several exquisite miniature species appear, only 1–2 in (2–5 cm) high, with white flowers. *R. seguieri* is one of the best, but *R. crenatus* and *R. traunfellneri* are similar. These are the ideal trough plants, but look at home in the scree with small neighbours. In late April and May *R. parnassifolius* usually flowers. This is another very variable species which ideally should be seen in flower when buying it, or should be grown from seed of a good clone. It forms a cluster of very dark rounded heart-shaped leaves with flower stems up to 8 in (20 cm), with several white flowers which again may have a pink tinge and which vary in size from the squinny to the magnificent! I am convinced that these all like rich soil, and even some well-rotted manure will not come amiss!

1. *Celmisia asteliifolia* (sun-loving/mid-season)

2. *Geranium* 'Lawrence Flatman' (sun-loving/mid-season)

3. *Sisyrinchium macounii album* (sun-loving/mid-season)

4. Rock garden with *Hypericum olympicum* and *Moltkia intermedia* (sun-loving/mid-season)

5. *Lithodora diffusa* 'Heavenly Blue' and *Penstemon scouleri albus* (sun-loving/mid-season)

Figure 5   Ranunculus parnassifolius

ANEMONE

This is another very variable genus. It again belongs to the buttercup family and the individual flowers of most species (excluding the pulsatillas, which have now been made a separate genus) bear a considerable resemblance to those of ranunculus species, but if anything the variety is even greater, from small bulbous plants to large border perennials.

Many of the bulbous anemones do best in shade and will be discussed later, but *Anemone blanda* in any of its varieties, blue, pink or white, will flourish in the sun, especially on chalky soils. I grow them with other bulbs such as scillas and chionodoxas and dwarf narcissi, or plant them beneath early shrubs, forsythia, corylopsis, magnolias, *Prunus tenella*, etc. The later-flowering bulbous anemones, which derive from *Anemone coronaria, A. hortensis* and *A. pavonia*, the 'De Caen' and 'St Bavo' anemones, are not generally taken seriously as alpines as they rarely prove soundly perennial. However, the species themselves and especially *A. fulgens* with brilliant scarlet flowers on 8 in (20 cm) stems, can make good groups in chalky southern gardens, even though I find them rather gaudy for the rock garden.

Apart from the early bulbs, in sun or shade, the most satisfactory anemones for the rock garden are *A. magellanica* and its allies, *A.* × *lesseri* and one or two species which are bordering on the over-large. There seem to be naming

21

problems with the first group! First and foremost is *Anemone magellanica* 'Major', a really excellent clump-forming plant with large pale yellow flowers on 6–8 in (15–20 cm) stems from late April onwards. It seems to flourish anywhere in sun or partial shade and is one of the most striking plants in my garden.

Some authorities state that *A. magellanica*, supposedly a South American species, is in fact *A. multifida*, a North American species. To add to the confusion, *A. baldensis* from North Italy seems similar, as does *A. drummondii*, again from North America. They are all easy to grow and have smaller flowers than *A. magellanica* 'Major', pale cream in colour. Forms of *A. multifida* that I have grown from American seed have very small flowers of an excellent deep rose colour, and *A. drummondii* as I saw it in the Rockies recently had a delicate blue flush on the outside of the petals, which does not seem obvious in cultivated plants. In conclusion, I would recommend *A. magellanica* 'Major' first and any of the others if you have space.

PULSATILLA

The separation of *Pulsatilla* from *Anemone* has removed from the latter the most useful group of all for the garden. What could be more beautiful than the large goblet-shaped flowers surrounded by silky hairs, on a plant which is easily grown on a variety of soils in any reasonably open situation? Later, the seedheads are as beautiful as the flowers and are long-lasting until they are carried away on the wind. They are almost identical with clematis seeds, globular heads of shining silky strands.

Pulsatilla vulgaris is the species usually grown and it appears in a variety of colour forms, from pale lavender to deep purple, shades of red, and white. It interbreeds freely so that, even if you start, as I would strongly recommend, with a large-flowered pale lavender form, preferably with plenty of hairs, a good bright red and a large-flowered white, you will soon have self-sown seedlings in every conceivable intermediate stage. The only way to get the best forms is to purchase them in flower – there are many poor reds and whites around as well as some excellent ones, so be selective and preferably keep your best blue well away from your best red! As far as their manner of growth is concerned there is less variation. All die down in winter, leaving a conspicuous clump of dead leaves which needs cutting hard back. In early spring the fern-like leaves unfurl rapidly and produce an abundance of buds covered with long silky hairs. The plants in my experience are long-lived and eventually take up a foot square of space, but are never invasive although the seedlings may be widespread, if you are lucky! They are robust and striking enough to be planted in groups, preferably of similar colour, in the front of a border to prolong its season, or they can play their part in the colour scheme of the rock garden, preferably not among the smallest plants, which can easily become covered with their leaves.

There are other pulsatillas which I find less easy to grow. The most beautiful perhaps is *Pulsatilla vernalis*, an exquisite small species with golden-haired stems and flowers which are white flushed with blue on the outside of the petals. This needs rich scree conditions and makes a marvellous alpine house plant.

The finest of all the pulsatillas and to many the most beautiful of the larger European alpines is *Pulsatilla alpina*, with 12 in (30 cm) stems of brilliant white widely open flowers. On acid soils in the Alps its place is taken by *P. alpina* var. *apiifolia*, sometimes offered as *P. alpina* var. *sulphurea*, identical except in colour, which is pale yellow. Alas, they are equally difficult in the garden although one very occasionally sees good plants. The best chance of success seems to be to plant very young plants and leave them undisturbed. I keep trying but have never produced a plant I was proud of!

CORYDALIS

This genus has become increasingly popular recently with the introduction of new species, and perhaps with more appreciation of some of the old favourites, so it deserves inclusion among the 'major alpine genera'.

Many of the species are bulbous but they make such an important contribution as alpines in the spring garden that I feel they should be described here. Several of the most exciting do best in shady conditions and will be considered later. For the sunny garden the most important bulbous species is *Corydalis solida* with its varieties. The name seems to cover a number of plants, but generally it applies to a very easily-grown and freely increasing species with attractive glaucous fern-like leaves in early spring and 6 in (15 cm) spikes of dainty long-spurred flowers in a somewhat muddy reddish-purple colour. The variety to look out for is 'George Baker' or any plant under the name of *Corydalis transylvanica*, a name that was once applied to 'George Baker' and still appears occasionally. This resembles *C. solida* in its attractive foliage, but the flowers are a marvellous shade of reddish-pink. It is so beautiful that we might expect it to be difficult, but in fact it has increased very freely in my garden in reasonably well-drained soil, in sun and in partial shade.

Corydalis caucasica var. *alba*, sometimes offered as *C. caucasica*, is a very beautiful white species now appearing in gardens. In my garden it has proved easy in a well-drained raised bed, seeding itself around gently into sunny and shady positions. It is only 2–3 in (5–7 cm) high with spikes of dangling white long-spurred flowers a little above the leaves. It flowers in early spring and quickly disappears below ground again. *Corydalis nobilis* flowers considerably later and is surprisingly little known for such an attractive plant. Planted two or three years ago in a raised bed, it is now 12 in (30 cm) high in flower, with typical glaucous leaves and rather dense spikes of deep yellow flowers, which have dark anthers and dark tips to the petals.

In complete contrast to these species, which die down soon after flowering, *Corydalis cheilanthifolia* looks good throughout the year, with delicate golden-bronze ferny leaves and spikes of yellow flowers off and on through the summer, after a main flush in late spring. It is undeniably beautiful, but its over-prolific seeding makes it a beautiful menace! it is one of those plants that cannot be dead-headed as the flowers tend to be tucked down among the leaves, so I am forever pulling up seedlings from unwanted situations. They come up very easily and I would hate to be without such an attractive plant!

It is probably safe to say that all of the species are beautiful and worth growing, but many new introductions are unproved or need careful cultivation under glass, often with a summer drying-off period. Two very easy species for a cold house are frustratingly difficult or short-lived in the garden. These are *C. wilsonii* and *C. tomentella*, both with a cluster of very glaucous leaves and beautiful yellow flowers. *C. tomentella* has the more attractive leaves as they are intensely grey and hairy.

Most corydalis species are easily raised from seed, but it is very important that seed should be sown fresh. The seed is usually ripe by the time the capsules are beginning to turn yellow and is rapidly lost if you leave it too long. Sow it immediately after collection and germination will be excellent, but germination of stored seed is poor.

Mainly under Glass

I have described briefly some of the most exciting alpine genera, but so far I have avoided those in which the majority of species need some protection under glass. Enthusiasts might consider these the elite, and anyone truly bitten by the alpine-growing bug will want to refer to a more specialised publication on the Alpine House for full information on them. I will describe a few easy species of each genus suitable for the open garden, and mention a few of the best needing at least a pane of glass over their heads in winter.

ANDROSACE

A fascinating genus of high alpines, many of which are cushion plants that will cover themselves in flower in the spring, but resent winter wet and therefore will not survive without some overhead protection. Typical examples are *Androsace vandellii*, *A. pyrenaica*, *A. cylindrica* and *A. hirtella*, with white flowers, and *A. ciliata*, with pink flowers.

Various species with larger rosettes are less tricky and will grow outside in the scree or as crevice plants between rocks, gradually forming a widening mat of hairy rosettes with short stems of several flowers in the spring. This general description covers such species as *A. carnea* with its various named varieties, *halleri*, *laggeri*, etc., *A. lanuginosa* with very hairy silvery rosettes, and *A. sarmentosa* (*A. primuloides*) with several varieties. All these have pink flowers and are quite easy in the situations suggested.

A. sempervivioides and *A. villosa* are also possible outside in very well-drained soil and are even more compact. *A. sempervivioides* forms a low mat of deep green rosettes and smothers itself with pink flowers every spring. *A. villosa* has much more hairy rosettes and white flowers on one inch (2 cm) stems, often with a red eye; *A. jacquemontii* is probably a variety of it and has deeper rose flowers.

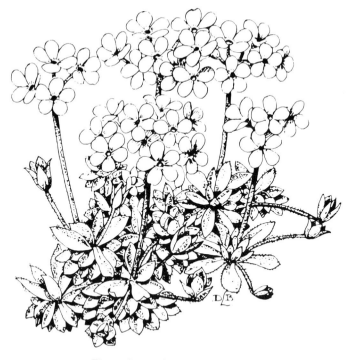

Figure 6   Androsace sarmentosa

Several beautiful Himalayan species have been introduced recently, which do better in partial shade and will be considered later.

The androsaces mentioned are very small plants only 1–2 in (2–5 cm) high and make ideal subjects for a trough apart from those described as needing overhead protection. In scree conditions on the rock garden or in a raised bed they need careful placing among other very small plants or the tiniest bulbs, to avoid them becoming overgrown and to keep the scale right. The small primula and gentian species described are ideal to extend the colour range. There are no yellow androsace species but *Vitaliana primulaeflora* is a very close ally. Until recently it was known as a species of *Douglasia*, but it is now threatened with inclusion in *Androsace*. This is a very easily grown plant that makes a carpet of small silver-edged rosettes, which always look attractive, and has a sprinkling of pure yellow flowers in spring. Look out for its variety *praetutiana*, which is possibly more compact and silvery and should be more floriferous.

Other douglasias are probably safer under glass, although I have found *D. laevigata* and its variety *ciliolata* reasonably long-lived in scree, very attractive cushion plants with green leaves and heads of deep rose flowers. *D. montana* with pink flowers and *D. nivalis* with deep purple flowers are decidedly more difficult, but very beautiful under glass.

DRABA

I was not sure where to put this genus because, although many species are easy to grow in the rock garden, the really outstanding plants need care with watering. They present no problems under glass, but are very difficult outside because of their resentment of winter wet. The best species here are *Draba mollissima*, *D. acaulis*, *D. longisiliqua* and *D. polytricha*, superb cushion plants with abundant yellow flowers which are stemless in *D. acaulis* but on one inch (2 cm) stems in the others.

Among the easier species are several very dwarf plants for association with other tiny alpines in the rock garden or as crevice plants. Several names will be found in catalogues, for example *D. aizoides*, *D. bryoides* and *D. bruniifolia*. All these have small rosettes of deep green leaves and short stems with typical yellow crucifer flowers and deserve a place among the saxifrages, primulas and gentians in the rock garden.

Mid-season (May–July)

In the previous section I described a selection of the more important alpines which flower in the spring. Together with bulbs and the earliest shrubs they will have been the most important source of colour in the garden, whereas from May onwards alpines become just one part of the major flowering season, first of shrubs, especially on acid soil, and later of border perennials.

In the rock garden or in raised beds devoted only to alpines, April and May are the most colourful months and are often followed by a gradual decline. I hope to show that there are plenty of other plants to keep the interest going even as late as September and October, although I must admit that colour is then more difficult to find, and foliage becomes increasingly important.

In the rest of the garden I feel that alpines are often neglected. The shrub enthusiast may be happy to leave bare soil along the front of beds, and also between the shrubs if these have been sensibly planted with an eye to their future development. These are ideal situations for the 'easy carpeters', for want of a better term, the sort of plants which do not need too much special soil preparation and are content with the conditions provided for the shrubs. In many such situations shade-lovers will be more appropriate and these will be described later, but whatever plants are used they will extend the season of interest of any borders. Bare soil may look tidy if enough time is devoted to it, but as far as I am concerned, it is wasted space!

In mixed borders, with perennials planted among the shrubs, it may well be that the only space for alpines is along the front, but they can still add greatly to the picture with a gradation of height from carpeters of an inch or two in front, through medium-sized perennials, to a backdrop of large shrubs and the more statuesque perennials and grasses.

I have suggested choosing plants which will be content with the normal border soil, but in order to give myself the maximum scope – my rock garden is never big enough – I frequently incorporate a generous amount of grit along the edges of all the borders, enabling me to grow some of the less vigorous plants which need good drainage.

Easy Carpeters

Here is a selection of the best species among the more important genera, with a few further suggestions in the tables at the back of the book. So many genera flower during the summer that it is best to take them alphabetically, rather than to follow the arrangement of the previous chapter.

ASTER AND ERIGERON

The differences between these genera are mainly botanical, so that it seems reasonable to consider them together. In practice, most asters are too large for our purposes, and *Erigeron* contains several good small species that are too delicate for the hurly-burly of a mixed border and will be described with that other elite of alpine daisies – the townsendias.

I must confess to a lack of enthusiasm for the larger 'Michaelmas daisies' even though they can provide good late colour if the varieties are well-chosen. *Aster amellus* varieties are a different matter, excellent medium-height perennials with a long season of fine pale to deep lavender flowers. They are far too big to consider here, but I grow them as a beautiful background to any of the diascias and dianthuses mentioned later, or to the white *Viola cornuta*.

Aster natalense is small enough and special enough for the rock garden but is easily-grown anywhere. In spite of its South African provenance it seems quite hardy here and makes rosettes of very dark green hairy leaves almost flat on the ground, with single blue daisies on 2 in (5 cm) stems. The others worth mentioning vary from 6–18 in (15–45 cm) in height, and all have typical lavender flowers. Look out for such names as *Aster alpinus*, *A. himalaicus* and *A. tibeticus*, to which might be added *A. sikkimense*, a fairly recent introduction. These may not seem very exciting to the alpine enthusiast, but they are colourful and combine well with the pink of the diascias or the yellow of oenotheras and hypericums.

Erigeron mucronatus deserves special mention as a useful 'weed', seeding itself madly around the garden, often to excess. I like it best where it puts itself into paving crevices or in retaining walls, even in poor dry conditions, producing an endless succession of small daisy flowers in shades from pink to white.

CAMPANULA

This is an enormous genus of plants from tiny alpine house treasures to the tallest and coarsest of perennials – invaluable in providing shades of blue and white throughout the summer. I shall consider the smaller treasures later and confine myself here to some of the easy species, less than 1 ft (30 cm) high, which most appeal to me as foreground plants.

The tiniest of these is *Campanula cochlearifolia*, with a running root, tiny spoon-shaped leaves and short stems of nodding bells, pale blue in the type plant but with several varieties available from nurseries; these may be white, or

Figure 7   Campanula cochlearifolia

a deeper shade of lavender, and may be single or double. They are so small that I grow them on the rock garden, but they are especially attractive when running through crevices in paving or walls.

Campanula carpatica and its various forms are ideal for foreground planting, whether among shrubs or perennials, and are so easy to grow that they are not generally thought of as alpines. They are all 6–12 in (15–30 cm) high, and a search in nurserymen's catalogues will produce varieties from white through pale lavender to deep purple. Their different shades can be used in different ways or they can be combined happily together in a group of their own. I grow several varieties along the front of a pair of borders devoted entirely to 'pastel shades' and silver foliage plants. These beds have been very successful, but I must confess that they are copied from the beautiful walled garden at Wakehurst Place, which is a symphony of soft colours from midsummer onwards.

While considering the most robust species I must mention the two greatest thugs, *C. portenschlagiana* (*C. muralis*) and *C. poscharskyana*. Their great vigour makes them useful for covering plenty of ground in difficult conditions or in a large retaining wall, where they will follow the aubretia and alyssum. Though of similar size they have very different flowers, deep bells in *C. portenschlagiana* and wide-open stars in *C. poscharskyana*. *Campanula garganica*, available in several slightly different forms, is similar to the latter but not quite so vigorous and not so likely to swamp any small neighbours. It is easy to underestimate how much more space some of these campanulas with spreading flowering shoots will take up during their long flowering and seeding season. They should be given a good haircut after flowering, or they can look a mess for the rest of the season.

˙ One of the best smaller campanulas is *C.* × *haylodgensis*, which has masses of dainty wide-open double lavender flowers on 4 in (10 cm) stems. It looks very special but is quite easily satisfied. Even better, in my estimation, is its pristine white form, identical except in colour. Another excellent plant which is more vigorous than it looks is *C. pilosa*, usually offered in its 'Major' form. This has small pale green rosettes of leaves and almost stemless flowers, upturned pale blue bells heavily shaded with white towards the base. Still considering the daintier species, *C. pulla* surprisingly is rarely seen in gardens in spite of its darkest blue flowers on short stems above tiny leaves. It is a gently running plant suitable for paving or the rock garden and is perhaps a little small for the border.

C. sarmatica, a small species for the front of the border, is not often seen although it is a long-lived perennial and easily grown from seed. It forms pleasing mounds of grey-green leaves with sprays of pale lavender flowers in May and June, up to 12–15 in (30–37 cm) high. Although monocarpic plants are not generally considered suitable as alpines, I cannot resist suggesting *Campanula incurva*, which has recently found its way into the trade. It resembles a miniature 'Canterbury bell' with equally large pale lavender upturned goblets, but these are carried on spreading semi-prostrate stems, each plant taking up perhaps a square foot of space. Do not forget to keep some seed, as it never proves perennial.

The native British 'harebell', *C. rotundifolia*, is worth growing in the garden, especially in its variety 'Olympica' with larger flowers. In my own garden I have a white form, which does not run but forms a good clump of the typical fine-leaved stems with a long succession of white flowers in August.

CONVOLVULUS

I hope I shall be forgiven by gardeners in colder climes for introducing two carpeting *Convolvulus* species, both of which are tender in northern counties, and one of which can become a menace – but what a beautiful menace! *Convolvulus sabaticus* (*C. mauretanicus*) would be an ideal carpeter, making a spreading mat of shoots from a central rootstock, with abundant stemless blue flowers during the summer, but alas it will not survive bad winters. Clones seem to vary in hardiness, so if you have a friend whose plant survives a hard winter, beg a cutting or two. It is easy to propagate and well worth overwintering young plants for safety's sake. *Convolvulus althaeoides*, usually in its form *tenuissimus* (*C. elegantissimus*) is a peerless beauty with narrow silver leaves and large pale pink flowers. Any traveller to the classical sites of Greece, which are often overrun with it, must have fallen in love with those marvellous flowers. I suspect my own experience is typical – I duly fell in love, acquired it on several occasions, but failed to establish it because we had a succession of diabolical winters. With perseverance it eventually became established and now I have a square yard or two and am forever discouraging it from spreading into the homes of more delicate plants. This is probably a losing battle, but from July onwards, when those pale pink flowers appear, all is forgiven!

DIANTHUS

This is a most important genus for any garden with a limy soil, but with hundreds of species and hybrids available, all of a suitable size for inclusion here, it is difficult to know how to treat it. The hybrid pinks in particular are frequently exhibited at RHS shows and can be seen in the collections of specialist nurserymen, so that a personal choice can be made. It must be said that although they all look fine when exhibited they do not always make ideal garden plants as they can rapidly lose vigour, unless they are propagated and replanted frequently. I have only grown a selection in my own garden, but a few of these have proved good perennials and are ideal foreground plants for a sunny place, with good grey leaves throughout the year and an excellent scent (usually) during the flowering season.

The hybrid 'Inchmery' has proved one of the best, providing after three or four years a carpet about 18 in (45 cm) square of healthy leaves only about 3 in (7 cm) high, with a profusion of pale pink semi-double flowers during June and July. 'Pike's Pink' is another excellent plant, not so quick-growing but building up into a mound several inches across with pale pink double flowers with a deeper eye. As a contrast to these, *Dianthus* 'Musgrave's Pink' makes a low carpet (like 'Inchmery') but has single white flowers with a broad green eye – always a happy combination. This is a surprisingly old hybrid, which seems to have retained its vigour. Another old hybrid worth seeking out is 'Spark', with deep green leaves and single flowers of intense scarlet. If you like this fearsome colour it is worth taking cuttings periodically to ensure its survival through hard winters.

Many of the *Dianthus* species need some care in a well-drained sunny site, but a few will certainly qualify as easy carpeters, notably *D. deltoides* and its various forms. They all make low ground-hugging mats of tiny green leaves, and have myriads of small short-stemmed flowers. These can be deep pink or white in the typical plant, but are white with a deep red eye in 'Brighteyes' and deep scarlet in 'Flashing Eyes'. Various other names will be found in catalogues.

Some species have deeply cut frilly flowers, and two of the easiest of these are *D. superbus* and *D. squarrosus*. *D. superbus* makes a lax cushion with pink flowers, whereas *D. squarrosus* makes a more dense mat of green leaves with pure white heavily scented flowers. Some of the smaller species will be considered later.

DIASCIA

Who would have thought five years ago that this would become such a popular genus of plants for general garden use? Although *Diascia cordata* and its hybrid 'Ruby Field' have been grown by alpine enthusiasts for many years, it is only recently that the more vigorous species have become widely grown. I well remember the excitement of first seeing a colour photograph of *Diascia rigescens* in *The Garden*, which must have sent every gardener rushing for their 'wants list'. It proved so easy to propagate that it reached many gardens within a couple of years, accompanied by a flow of other species.

Diascias all flourish in a sunny position with adequate moisture and have flowers of an unusually clear shade of pink, which combines happily with silver foliage plants or with the blues and purples of my pastel border from mid-summer onwards. From the gardener's viewpoint few plants are perfect and the diascias are slightly tender. It seems to take a very harsh winter to kill them outright, but they are likely to be cut back to near ground level by persistent temperatures below 18°F. On the other hand, they grow rapidly in the spring and are easily propagated, so a rooted cutting overwintered under glass may well make a plant a foot across, flowering abundantly, by late summer.

Most of the species resemble each other closely and make a mound of soft stems with pale green leaves up to 12 in (30 cm) high, with spikes of pale pink flowers which first appear in June and often continue until the autumn. The most widely grown and certainly the most tender here in Kent is *D. rigescens* with rather stiff upright stems of toothed leaves and taller flower spikes than most. For general use in a mixed border I prefer the very similar species *D. elegans*, *D. felthamii* and *D. vigilis* which are lower growing and hardier. My own favourite is *D. vigilis*, which has flowers of a paler more delicate shade of pink. Another excellent species is *D. integerrima*, which has a definitely running rootstock and very narrow leaves on upright stems but similar spikes of pink flowers.

Smaller than these are the low carpeting plants *D. cordata* and *D. barberiae* and the excellent very hardy hybrid 'Ruby Field', which will give a similar effect to those mentioned but at a lower level.

ERYSIMUM (CHEIRANTHUS)

Most of the perennial wallflowers belong strictly to the genus *Erysimum*, but they may still be found under *Cheiranthus* in catalogues. They form a useful group of plants flowering in early summer in a range of colours from pale cream, through yellow and orange, to purple. Although often short-lived and a little tender, they are easy to propagate and, apart from enjoying sunshine, are very unfussy with regard to soil requirements. Most of them in general cultivation are hybrids and only the smaller ones are considered here, although *E. linifolium* and its varieties, and such plants as 'Rufus', 'Wenlock Beauty', 'Harpur Crewe', all 1–2 ft (30–60 cm) high, are excellent mixed border plants.

The best of the low carpeting varieties of *Erysimum* are too vigorous for a place in the average rock garden, quickly spreading to a foot or more wide, but can make a colourful edging to a herbaceous or shrub border before the main flush of flower begins.

One of the easiest and a hardy long-lived perennial is 'Orange Flame', under 6 in (15 cm) high with masses of bright orange flowers in May and June, a vivid colour which is not too easy to place except with yellow or deep purple flowers. 'Jubilee Gold' is a pleasanter colour, pale yellow with deep brownish-purple buds. It is a little taller and just as vigorous as 'Orange Flame'. 'Moonlight' is similar, with even paler flowers lacking the contrast of the dark buds. *Erysimum concinnum* is occasionally offered in catalogues. This species is a little taller, generally 9–12 in (23–30 cm), with spikes of pale cream flowers, always a useful colour in the garden. Like all these wallflowers it is better deadheaded after flowering, when it should produce a later flush of flowers. However, it comes true from seed, so it may be worthwhile retaining a few heads until it is ripe.

EUPHORBIA

Most of the spurges are too big to be considered here, but at least three qualify as easy plants under a foot high. First and foremost is *Euphorbia myrsinites* with prostrate stems of fleshy grey-green leaves carrying at their tips heads of bright yellow bracts and flowers which, like all the euphorbias, remain in good condition for several weeks.

E. cyparissias is mentioned only to be condemned, as it is a highly invasive runner only fit for the poorest of hot dry conditions. *E. segueriana* var. *niciciana* has rather similar upright stems of tiny pale grey-green leaves and heads of similar bracts in June and July. Far from being invasive it tends to be short-lived, at least in my own garden. I was sad to lose it, as it is one of the most beautiful of all the smaller spurges and formed a good group with the taller *Eryngium variifolium* and a variegated weigela.

GERANIUM

This is a massive genus and one of the most useful to the gardener, especially in providing ground-covering plants for sun or light shade, most of which are too large and vigorous to be classed as alpines. Among those preferring a more open position are several excellent dwarf species and hybrids which are easy to grow, as well as a few needing more specialised conditions.

Geranium dalmaticum is one of the best of the small carpeting species. It will take a year or two to attain a foot wide mat of small rounded pale green leaves with hundreds of short stems of pale pink flowers. There is an attractive white form whose only fault is that it always has a slight pink flush at the base of the petals.

Geranium renardii is one of my favourite species. It forms a mound of velvety grey-green heavily veined leaves which are beautiful at all seasons, and has flowers on 4 in (10 cm) stems in an unusual shade of palest lavender heavily veined with brownish purple. Our native *Geranium sanguineum* is a little tall, but its subspecies *lancastriense* is a first-class low carpeter, only an inch or two high with pale pink flowers. It has given rise to several hybrids of which 'Shepherd's Warning' is one of the best, a deeper rose colour. *G. sanguineum* 'Album' is a vigorous plant that will provide a patch of pure white in front of a border or can be used to hide the bare stems of some leggy perennials or shrubs.

I have used it here around the bases of several of the large roses, such as the pink 'Lady Curzon' and *Rosa californica* var. *plena*, and also as an edging to part of the pastel borders.

Geranium cinereum and its subspecies and hybrids form a group of some of the best alpine geraniums. They do best in well-drained soil, but seem to be perfectly happy in reasonable loam if it is not too heavy. *G. cinereum* itself has rosettes of grey-green leaves and large deep pink flowers with darker veins. Its subspecies *subcaulescens*, often offered as a species, is very different in flower colour, a vivid magenta with a dark eye. The same colour is seen in the widely-grown *Geranium psilostemon* on a much larger scale. Magenta seems to be a dirty word in many circles, but if you like the colour it is seen at its strongest (best?) in this geranium. It makes a startling contrast to white flowers, growing in my own garden next to the grey leaved white flowered native *Silene maritima* – definitely a talking point! Try it also with the greenish-yellow of euphorbias. Three good hybrids derived from *G. cinereum* are 'Apple Blossom', 'Ballerina' and the more recent 'Lawrence Flatman'. All have similar silvery leaves, but in 'Apple Blossom' the flowers are clear pink with the faintest of veining, whereas in 'Ballerina' the colour is a lilac-pink with heavy reddish veining. 'Laurence Flatman' has the most striking flowers of all with very dark reddish-purple veining on the petals.

Geranium traversii, usually seen in its form 'Elegans', is a singularly beautiful plant only suitable for warm gardens. In Kent I find it is frequently killed by the cold winters, but usually leaves a few self-sown seedlings which appear in the spring. It forms a low mat of silvery leaves and large rounded very pale pink flowers for months on end. A well-drained soil will probably help it to survive the cold, although it grows well enough in ordinary soil. It is certainly worth collecting some seed each year before its trigger mechanism flings it around the garden.

Catalogues sometimes offer *Geranium procurrens* as 'useful groundcover' for any situation, but it should really carry a health warning as a dangerous menace, which in at least one National Trust garden could only be eliminated by a potent weedkiller. The flowers are an attractive very deep purple, probably the darkest of any geranium, but the shoots not only root at every node but seem to produce deep tap roots at every node. My advice would be to avoid it except in the wildest places. Instead, grow its recently produced hybrid 'Anne Folkard', with flowers only a little paler and long trailing shoots which will climb through other plants and never seem to root downwards. It flowers from July onwards and I particularly like to see it scrambling through the later euphorbias, such as *E. schillingii*, *E. wallichiana* or *E. longifolia*, or among the larger golden-leaved hostas.

GYPSOPHILA
Although this is a small genus containing some popular medium-sized border plants, it also provides two useful species for the front of the border which will make spreading carpets flowering abundantly during June. The species usually

grown is *Gypsophila repens*, with several named varieties offered by nurserymen. It makes a low mat of tiny-leaved bluish stems, above which appear abundant small flowers in shades of pink or white, excellent in front of some of the larger blue or white campanulas.

The other equally easily grown species is *G. cerastioides*. This is very different, with soft hairy pale green leaves in a low mat and rather larger white flowers with brownish veining. Like *G. repens* it generally flowers in late May or June.

HYPERICUM

This is a large and diverse genus with species from the tiniest mat-formers to the largest shrubs. Many hypericums are low-growing easy plants suitable for inclusion here, but unfortunately they are not generally as hardy as one might wish, especially on heavy soils. There is surprisingly little variation in colour, which is usually a bright yellow, associating best with hot reds and oranges or deep purple, but a few species are a pale creamy-yellow, which I find useful to separate the hot colours from the more pastel shades. The most valuable species, because it is the hardiest, is probably *Hypericum olympicum* with its excellent pale variety 'Citrinum'. Both are easily grown and gradually build up during June or July into a spreading carpet 3–4 in (7–10 cm) high of small glaucous leaves and large flowers with a boss of prominent stamens.

Hypericum orientale is less often seen. It has more upright branches with deep green leaves and smaller dark yellow flowers, and seems completely hardy in Kent. Its one fault, other than a rather harsh colour, is that it tends to seed itself around too freely. There are several more dainty and, unfortunately, more tender low-growing species. Two of the best are *H. reptans*, a ground-hugging mat with small yellow flowers opening from attractive reddish buds, and *H. trichocaulon*, which is similar but larger in all its parts. *H. empetrifolium* is a more woody plant with upright stems and tiny leaves, but is low-growing in its variety 'Prostratum'. These three plants are easy enough to grow, but it may be safer to keep them on the rock garden so that they get the benefit of the best possible drainage.

Some of the other small *Hypericum* species are more suitable for the alpine house and will be mentioned in the tables.

LAMIUM

This usually means *Lamium maculatum*, a useful ground-cover for difficult places in sun or shade, especially in its best foliage forms like 'Beacon Silver' or 'White Nancy', but too rapidly spreading to accept here. *L. orvala* is an interesting border plant of medium size, and the only two species really worth considering here are *L. armenum*, a remarkably beautiful and difficult species, and *L. garganicum* var. *pictum*, which might be considered its poor relation but is definitely worth growing if you can find one of its best forms. It does not root as it goes, like the coarser lamiums, but spreads from a central rootstock to

34

make a plant about 6 in (15 cm) high and a foot across in a couple of years. The flowers are pale pink heavily streaked and spotted with purple.

LITHODORA
Many years ago there was an 'opinion poll' to find the best five alpines, and it was won by *Lithospermum diffusum* 'Heavenly Blue', its name now changed to *Lithodora diffusa*. It may be less popular now but is still one of the most admired plants in this garden, flowering next to the pale white *Penstemon scouleri* var. *albus* and beneath the creamy-white broom *Cytisus albus*. Unfortunately it resents lime, but in sun or light shade on an acid soil it will make an extensive carpet of small dark hairy leaves completely covered in June in flowers of that perfect blue seen in gentians, in *Salvia patens*, and in few other plants. Give it plenty of humus and top dress it with leaf mould or peat when it starts getting leggy and it will flourish for years. *L. diffusa* 'Grace Ward' is similar, and possibly a little more vigorous.

The only other species which might be considered an easy-carpeter is *L. oleifolium*, but this is really one for well-drained sunny scree conditions where it will run about underground, gradually building up a cluster of stems with glaucous grey-green leaves and the typical bright blue flowers, not in the same abundance as *L. diffusa* varieties.

OENOTHERA
I find the smaller evening primroses irresistible, especially after seeing them flowering in all shapes and sizes in the Nevada desert, where most of them seemed to have pure white flowers and interesting grey leaves, admittedly a little large generally for the rock garden. Unfortunately many of them are not in cultivation and we must be content with some tall perennials, often short-lived and yellow-flowered, and a few good alpines with exceptionally large flowers which look spectacular in the foreground of a mixed border or as rock garden plants. The fine white-flowered *Oenothera caespitosa* has big rosettes of hairy leaves and, with me, seems to do best planted on its side in a retaining wall. Even there it is never very long-lived.

The only real carpeters are *O. missouriensis* and *O. riparia*. The former has long spreading stems from the central rootstock, which can cover up to a yard square in good conditions. Towards the tips, large saucer-shaped yellow flowers appear during several weeks at midsummer; these are 2–3 in (5–7 cm) across and need placing among larger shrubs or at the top of a wall for the proportions to be right. Although individual flowers only last twenty-four hours they do open during the day! *O. riparia*, strictly a subspecies of the upright *O. tetragona*, has semi-prostrate stems and makes a mound of shoots, much smaller in the leaf and with flowers half the size. It is one of the best summer-flowering easy alpines.

If you see *Oenothera speciosa* with beautiful pale pink flowers 2 in (5 cm) across on 12 in (30 cm) stems – resist it. I had great difficulty acquiring it and now find it an even greater menace than *Convolvulus althaeoides*. I only hope it is sufficiently tender to be killed by an average winter. It comes from Mexico, so it might be!

OSTEOSPERMUM (DIMORPHOTHECA)

The alpine purist will disapprove of the inclusion of this genus on the grounds that osteospermums are tender and too easily grown, but I find them among the most valuable long-flowering plants in the garden. After a series of devastating winters in Kent with temperatures down to 0°F, at least two species have proved themselves perfectly hardy, and others will survive mild winters. They are so easy to propagate that I always keep a few rooted cuttings under glass to grow away fast in the spring.

In any reasonable soil in full sun they grow rapidly and flower all through the summer, most of them taking up too much space for the rock garden or anywhere in association with tiny plants other than spring bulbs, which will flower and die down before the osteospermums have started their main sideways growth. In fact, this is an excellent way of using them as they can be planted widely among bulbs and then cut back hard if necessary as the bulbs are coming into growth.

The two most important species are *Osteospermum jucundum* (*barberiae*) with deep rose flowers and *O. ecklonis* with white flowers faintly tinged with palest violet which shades the outside of the petals. Both of these have survived severe winters in my garden, especially in their dwarf forms. *O. jucundum* has a very compact form 'Compacta', small enough for the rock garden. The best form of *O. ecklonis* is 'Prostrata', a much more rapidly-growing plant but not reaching more than 8 in (20 cm) high.

I think these are the best choice if you are looking for low-growing hardy plants. There are now lots of named varieties, many of them more upright and more tender, but all admirable gap fillers for the border, easy to keep going from cuttings. One which deserves special mention is 'Weetwood', similar to *O. ecklonis* 'Prostrata' but of more compact growth, which is relatively untried but seems to me to be just as hardy.

PENSTEMON

Osteospermums may be dubious 'alpines', but in the genus *Penstemon* we have everything from true compact hardy alpines to large perennials, many of them doubtfully hardy. It seems to me to be a genus of tremendous potential which we are only just beginning to explore, especially for plants of medium to small size for the mixed border. Some of the best small-growing species likely to be available are described here, but bear in mind that enthusiasts are constantly receiving seed of new species worthy of trial.

Among the species which have been most successful in my own garden I would put *Penstemon scouleri* 'Albus' high on my list of favourite alpines. This is a shrubby species that does not seem to get much higher than 10 in (25 cm) but spreads gradually sideways, layering itself as it goes, so that it can be just

Figure 8   Penstemon hirsutus

included as a carpeter. It flowers generally in May, so abundantly that it appears as a mound of pure white trumpets with hardly a leaf to be seen. *P. scouleri* itself seems less vigorous and has flowers of a very wishy-washy pale lavender, at least in the only plant I have grown. It is difficult not to doubt whether they represent the same species.

Considerably lower growing than *P. scouleri*, *P. cardwellii* has proved itself an excellent absolutely hardy species, with quite large deepest purple flowers. After about five years of cold winters this has made a low mat 4 in (10 cm) high and 2 ft (60 cm) across. *P. procerus* var. *tolmei* is rather similar in habit but grows about 6 in (15 cm) high. It flowers much less freely here, with short spikes of deep blue flowers. There is also a yellow-flowered form that is distinctly taller with pale yellow flowers.

Many of the penstemons have blue flowers but the quality of the blue varies considerably even among different clones of the same species. Frequently there is a pink tinge towards the base of the flower, which detracts a little from it. This applies to a variable extent in *P. procerus* var. *tolmei*, and also in *P. alpinus* and *P. virens*, which look bluer in the wild than in the garden. *Penstemon alpinus*, in spite of its name, is a rather loose-growing species at least 12 in (30 cm) high in flower, whereas I find *P. virens* is keeping promisingly compact; definitely a species to consider for the rock garden.

Penstemon whippleanus is another very hardy species that has spread quite quickly into a 2 ft (60 cm) wide mat, not more than 6 in (15 cm) high except when it flowers. The spikes are only a little taller, each carrying a cluster of typical tubular flowers of an unusual shade of dusky-purple. It is not as floriferous as some species, but its dusky colour makes a good contrast to brighter pinks and yellows.

P. hirsutus and its variety 'Pygmaeus' have the added attraction of purple foliage. The type plant grows to about 6 in (15 cm) high, with its flower spikes 3–4 in (7–10 cm) above the leaves, which are deep purple, though varying with conditions. The flowering stems carry a dense spike of small tubular flowers, deep violet in colour with white at the throat. The more popular 'Pygmaeus' is a miniature only 2–3 in (5–7 cm) high with much paler, dare I suggest rather wishy-washy flowers, and is not such a good plant as the type.

Some of the other easily-grown penstemons are more shrubby in habit and will be considered in the mid-season section (see p. 54).

THYMUS

I am hesitant to bring the thymes into this section although they are without doubt the easiest of carpeting plants for a sunny position, even in poor soils. Their one fault is that of excessive exuberance, and anyone planting them should bear in mind that they will cover a lot of ground, rooting as they go, with a short period of glory at mid-summer when their carpets of tiny leaves become completely covered in flower, from white to shades of pink and purple. A choice can be made from catalogues which offer a considerable number of varieties. These remarks apply mainly to *Thymus serpyllum*.

Some of the more upright shrubby species are as easy to grow but are more readily controlled, including those with silver or gold variegated leaves. *Thymus × citriodorus* var. 'Argenteus' and several named variables like 'Silver Queen' have white variegated leaves and grow to about 9 in (22 cm) in height. They are reasonably hardy and are among my favourite dwarf foliage plants throughout the year, with the pinkish flowers making little contribution in the summer. In fact, as these flowers die it is probably as well to prune the plant hard to keep the foliage in pristine condition. The golden leaved varieties are equally good as permanent foliage plants, although I feel that the flowers detract a little at the height of summer. *T. citriodorus* 'Aureus' was probably the first of these but several named varieties are now available from nurseries.

One other shrubby species deserves special mention, the rarely grown *T. mastichina*. This again is a hardy species with grey leaves, but it is more upright in habit and the flowers are the main attraction, abundant fluffy round heads of tiny white flowers for several weeks in July and August. This is another plant which benefits from a haircut, otherwise going through a definitely tatty phase after flowering.

Some of the finest *Thymus* species are more suitable for the alpine house than for the foreground of a mixed border and these will be considered later.

VIOLA

This is a very large and popular genus, all of a suitable size to be thought of as 'alpines', but I propose to miss out most of the pansies and violettas obtainable from specialist growers and concentrate on the species, all of them beautiful and many of them longer-lived perennials than the popular hybrids.

Many of the species grow better in partial shade and others are tricky plants for the alpine house and scree and will be described later. However, at least two species are without any fads or fancies and will carpet the ground in full sun or in partial shade among shrubs, maybe with a slight preference for some shade. I find that *Viola cornuta* in its various forms is the ideal easy violet, with a long flowering period and a delightful way of sowing itself gently and in the right places. It is easy enough to pull up too! *Viola cornuta* itself has deep lavender flowers, but varieties with darker flowers, for example 'Purpurea', can be found and also paler flowers nearer to a true blue as in 'Belmont Blue'. 'Lilacina' is an unusual shade of pinkish-lilac, and 'Alba' is an excellent pure white which seems to come true from seed. As a lover of white flowers I think 'Alba' is my favourite variety, whether as a foreground plant in a mixed border (where it can be used to separate those adjacent clashes which I am always perpetrating inadvertently) or rambling about at the base of shrub roses or other shrubs. It seems to enjoy climbing up into their lower branches like some of the geraniums, thus helping to cover bare stems. *Viola cornuta* itself behaves in the same way and the two look beautiful together. There are dwarf forms, named 'Compacta', of both the lavender and the white, excellent for a smaller-scale planting. I find that they hybridise with the type plant, and larger and larger progeny gradually appear around the original – probably my fault for not keeping them well apart, but I do grow a lot of *Viola cornuta* and have not the heart to cull them!

I have a love–hate relationship with *Viola labradorica*. It is beautiful with its purple leaves and small purple flowers, and it will grow in sun or shade, but it spreads rapidly underground and seeds excessively, exploding its seeds far and wide. I have now relegated it to a few difficult dry areas and try to remove its maddening seedlings from elsewhere.

Three other species which are not truly carpeting plants tend to produce the same effect by their profuse seeding, at least in well-drained soil. They are the rare *V. corsica* with large pale blue flowers on 4 in (10 cm) stems, *V. jooi*, a smaller plant with rounded leaves and small pinkish-lavender flowers, and *V. pedatifida*, a very easy free-seeding species with deeply cut leaves and small violet flowers on 4 in (10 cm) stems. All these are better avoided in a well-made rock garden, as they add considerably to the weeding. It is better to let them loose among shrubs or larger perennials.

Mid-season Main Alpine Genera
AQUILEGIAS

Everybody loves columbines with their beautiful leaves and dainty flowers. Most of them are easy to grow and can be used anywhere, the larger species in groups in the herbaceous border, or among shrubs if they are not too heavily shaded, the smaller species on the rock garden or in the foreground of borders if you have sufficient plants to make reasonable groups. They really have only one fault: they interbreed prolifically unless the species are kept well apart. As a result I sometimes find that what was expected to be a spectacular group of one species is only a disappointing hotch-potch of mixed hybrids.

I shall only consider some of the best small species here – those unlikely to grow more than 12 in (30 cm) high in an open situation. If possible, I like to plant several of these small aquilegias together in a group, preferably of three or five among other alpines, or as many as possible to make real impact in front of a mixed border.

There are several blue-flowered dwarf species ideal for the rock garden. Their nomenclature is somewhat confused and I see that some publications still list *Aquilegia akitensis* and *A. flabellata* separately, although they are now considered by botanists to be the same species *A. flabellata*. Under either of these names you can obtain an exquisite plant with glaucous leaves and large blue flowers with long curved spurs, generally on stems of about 4–6 in (10–15 cm) , although the height varies in different forms. The central tube of the flower may have a greater or lesser amount of white. I find that the exceptionally fine pure white form of this species usually comes true from seed, as indeed does the type itself. *Aquilegia bertolonii* is a similar very neat blue-flowered plant, which is easy in sunny conditions.

There are several species from America with long-spurred red flowers with a yellow centre. Most of these are near to or over our size limit, but are lovely plants to group among shrubs. Names are again confused but *A. canadensis*, *A. truncata*, *A. formosa* and *A. eximia* should all be of this colouring. The uncommon *A. barnebyana* is the one real dwarf, but is not often obtainable.

Another colour to be found in aquilegias is a deep chocolate-purple. *A. atrata* and *A. grata* both have flowers of this colour, the latter in my experience keeping rather smaller, just within our limit. Another species with flowers of an unusual sombre hue is *A. viridiflora*. This has 8–12 in (20–30 cm) stems, carrying several small flowers that are a strange combination of dark green and purple – a fascinating plant to grow, but remember that the flowers are lost if a group is placed in front of dark evergreens.

Although not strictly an aquilegia, *Semiaquilegia ecalcarata* seems to fit in well here with its dainty reddish-purple flowers, several to a stem, very similar in habit to *A. viridiflora* but generally less tall – a beautiful plant easily grown from seed.

During the last few years I have been growing two superb species which have been introduced from the Himalayas and these seem to be settling reasonably well in cultivation, preferring a well-drained humus-rich soil in a little shade in this dry garden. First, there is the very dwarf *A. nivalis* with spurless dark blue flowers with an almost black centre, a most striking combination. In contrast, *A. fragrans* varies from 6–18 in (15–45 cm) high and has short-spurred cream-coloured flowers, occasionally with a tinge of blue, and usually with an excellent fragrance.

There are several dwarf species generally grown in the alpine house but which are quite possible in scree conditions in the open. In its best forms *Aquilegia scopulorum* is the most beautiful of all, with very long-spurred flowers, which are usually blue, but for several years I have grown a very dwarf form with exquisite pale pink flowers with a white centre. The taller forms are not quite so attractive but *A. saximontana* is a good dwarf with much shorter spurs and a yellow centre, which also grows in the Rockies and is occasionally available from nurseries.

CAMPANULA

Many of the more vigorous *Campanula* species have already been described, especially those capable of major impact among shrubs or larger perennials (see p. 27), but this is a huge genus and there is a wealth of small species which will be better appreciated among plants of their own size. Some may need extra drainage, or in very few cases alpine house treatment.

One of my favourites is the very dainty *Campanula arvatica*, a real miniature carpeter which runs gently underground. It appreciates plenty of drainage and full sun and will then form an inch-high mat of tiny leaves with abundant small deep violet-blue flowers in summer. The recently introduced hybrid 'Joe Elliott' is another of my favourite campanulas, with a similar habit of growth but with larger rosettes of leaves and fine upturned blue bells. So far, I am not convinced that it will prove as soundly perennial as *C. arvatica* but it is undoubtedly a very good new addition to the smaller campanulas. *Campanula raineri* likes similar conditions and has even larger and wider open bells on 2 in (5 cm) stems. *C. waldsteiniana* is another dainty late-flowering species only 4–6 in (10–15 cm) high, forming a clump of small-leaved upright stems tipped with deep violet starry flowers. I grew it from seed collected in Turkey and was delighted that in spite of its delicate appearance it is quite easy to grow.

There are several dwarf white campanulas including the beautiful double white form of *C.* × *haylodgensis*, named 'Warley White'. Quite different in habit is *C. planiflora* (*C. nitida*) 'Alba', with rosettes of very dark green leaves and upright 6–8 in (15–20 cm) spikes of outward-facing wide open flowers. The type plant is similar but pale blue in colour, and they are both micro-forms of the very common tall *C. persicifolia*. Unfortunately, seed from *C. planiflora* usually produces *C. persicifolia*. Some authorities state that this is always the case, but I find that quite a proportion of self-sown seedlings come true, and are easily recognisable with their broader darker leaves, so that the remainder can be weeded out quickly, as they are far too vigorous for a choice position.

Campanula betulifolia is often seen as an alpine house plant, but I have found it easy in a sunny site in the rock garden, seeding itself freely. It gradually makes a spreading mat of reddish-backed toothed leaves and has masses of large bell-shaped white flowers tinged to a greater or lesser degree with pink. This pink tinge is particularly noticeable in *C. finitima*, which is probably a

41

subspecies of *C. betulifolia*. Completely different again is 'Mist Maiden' with upright stems of tiny leaves bearing abundant small white flowers over a long period, so that it makes a white mound 6–8 in (15–20 cm) high.

Three campanula species are among my favourite alpine house plants, and can be tried in a scree or trough: *C. morettiana* and its white form, making very compact domes of hairy rosettes with large upturned bells, *C. zoysii*, a low-running plant, which has pale blue bells curiously puckered at their mouths and which is every slug's favourite food, and finally *C. cashmeriana*. This is an easy plant under glass, with grey leaves and lavender flowers, but it rarely survives the winter outside, unlike *C. zoysii*, which can be grown in a scree if only you can keep the predators at bay!

CELMISIA

This is a fascinating genus from Australasia. All celmisias have evergreen leaves and white daisy flowers, but otherwise display a remarkable diversity, from tiny carpeters to large rosettes of foot-long leaves. Most come from mountain areas with a high summer humidity, and for this reason they seem to grow much better in gardens with a high rainfall. Here in the South East I have had some success by growing them in the peat garden in partial shade and watering them frequently during dry spells. In the West and North they will grow well in full sun, given a reasonably humus-rich well-drained soil. Many species are available from specialist nurseries and seed lists, and any of them are worth trying, but in view of their rather special requirements, I shall confine myself here to a limited number of the most distinct.

The easiest of the low-growing carpeting species is *C. bellidiodes*, which makes an inch-high mat of tiny glossy dark green leaves, above which in early summer appears a sprinkling of small white daisy flowers on one inch (2.5 cm) stems.

Celmisia argentea and *C. sessiliflora* are two of the most exciting miniatures, but I wish they were easier to grow. *C. argentea* has intensely silver rosettes, making a low mound with large white flowers. In *C. sessiliflora* the rosettes are larger with a hint of green in the silver and very large stemless daisies – a striking plant when it is well-grown. I am convinced that they hate being under glass during the summer and that they are more likely to be successful in a raised bed or trough in rich scree conditions, perhaps with glass protection in winter if that can be arranged.

Celmisia gracilenta generally grows to about 6 in (15 cm) and has rosettes of very narrow green leaves, often striped across with brown markings, and typical daisies about one inch (2.5 cm) across. This has been one of the most successful species in a small bed that I have devoted to Australasian plants, a bed that only gets full sun in the middle of the day. It grows beside the even more beautiful Australian species *C. asteliifolia*, with narrow very silver leaves and abundant flowers in summer. With pratias and the little *Geranium sessilifolium* they grow along a path with a background of larger olearias,

Figure 9   Celmisia gracilenta

coprosmas and leptospermums, which suffer direly during cold winters while the foreground plants are unscathed.

C. ramulosa and *C. walkeri* have a more shrubby habit, gradually building up to 6–8 in (15–20 cm) high, with dark green leaves and the typical flowers on short stems. *C. hectori* and *C. angustifolia* make rosettes of intermediate size, their leaves 2–4 in (5–10 cm) long and flower spikes 6–8 in (15–20 cm). *C. angustifolia* is not often seen and can have either greyish-green or more silver leaves.

The bigger species are very striking with their large hairy green leaves with white or brownish felted backs. The largest of these is *C. semicordata*, often available as *C. coriacea*. Its leaves can be a foot or more long and are covered with white hairs in addition to the white felting on their backs. The large white daisies are carried on 12–18 in (30–45 cm) stems. *C. spectabilis* is similar, with leaves only a little smaller. Both species are quite easy to grow and are among the most spectacular evergreen foliage plants of medium size.

43

DELPHINIUM

Although the name conjures up a picture of magnificent large border plants, there are several excellent dwarf species available, and others are being introduced by seed, especially from the Himalayas and the USA. Unfortunately only a few appear in catalogues at present, and the seed lists of the specialist societies are a better source for any gardener wanting to grow a good range.

Delphinium tatsienense is the dwarf species most frequently available. It grows about 12 in (30 cm) high when in flower, with spikes of small brilliant blue flowers. It is reasonably perennial and easily raised from seed, so a group can be planted to give a fine splash of colour, the same intense blue as the best of the gentians. *Delphinium cashmerianum* is sometimes available, but unfortunately two plants are offered under this name. The true species seems to be short-lived, has broad-lobed leaves and two or three flowers on a stem, whereas the plant I first acquired under this name is even better than *D. tatsienense*, similar in colour but more compact and floriferous with somewhat similar narrow leaves. *D. brunonianum* is a recent introduction from the Himalayas with large grey-blue very hairy flowers above broad hairy leaves. It is proving quite easy to grow, but varies considerably in height from 6–18 in (15–45 cm).

Delphinium nudicaule is an American species with orange to red flowers, very variable in height. It is a spectacular plant but I find it very short-lived, like its even taller relation *D. cardinale*, which has flowers of a brilliant red colour.

DIANTHUS

Earlier I described a few of the most vigorous species of this very large genus. There remain a wealth of small-growing species, which are ideal for the sunny rock garden in well-drained soil. They can be the backbone of any rock garden on chalk or limestone, and I have feelings of guilt when I consider how little use I have made of them in more than forty years of gardening – admittedly always on acid soil. Perhaps one day I shall live on the chalk and a major compensation will be the ability to grow a large collection of dianthus species! Lime is not essential for them and I have grown enough to have some favourites, which I list here as a modest beginning for any collection.

What more appropriate species to start with than *Dianthus alpinus*. This makes a cushion of dark green leaves with masses of deep rose flowers in early summer. There are several other striking clones available, of which my favourites are 'Joan's Blood' with deepest crimson flowers, and 'Alba' with equally beautiful white flowers. They all need good drainage and even then tend to be short-lived – at least they are in my garden! They come reasonably true from seed and can also be propagated from cuttings.

Dianthus glacialis and *D. neglectus* (*D. pavonius*) are very similar to *D. alpinus* but are said to be lime-hating, at least in the wild. *D. callizonus* is another species with a reputation for being short-lived, but I find it no more difficult than the two previously mentioned. It makes a laxer cushion and has

Figure 10   Dianthus alpinus

reddish-pink flowers with a striking line of deeper markings a third of the way up each petal. There are several even neater species with small pink flowers, including *D. freynii* and *D. microlepis*.

If you like 'vegetable hedgehogs' *Dianthus erinaceus* is a worthwhile acquisition. It was introduced from a Turkish collection some twenty years ago and has proved remarkably tolerant and long-lived, making very large low cushions of very sharply-pointed rosettes. Unfortunately, flowering is very sparse – two or three moderate-sized pale pink flowers per square foot (0.09^2) if you are lucky!

Every gardener likes something unusual, so perhaps I should include *Dianthus knappii*. This is a short-lived plant that forms a loose cluster of tall flowering stems, with little other growth, unfortunately. Each stem is topped with a cluster of small flowers, which are a delightful clear lemon yellow in colour. Keep it growing from seed!

EDRAIANTHUS AND WAHLENBERGIA

The names seem muddled in these genera and are used somewhat haphazardly in catalogues. They are closely allied to campanulas, and most of them have blue bell-shaped flowers. They are often short-lived but are easily raised from seed, and I feel that their delicate beauty makes them worth persevering with.

The outstanding plant of the two genera is one of my favourite alpines – *Edraianthus pumilio*, which forms a neat mound of silvery-green narrow leaves, only one inch (2.5 cm) high, on which sit the large violet-blue flowers during May and June. This is an outstanding alpine for a very well-drained spot among other small treasures, or in the alpine house.

Edraianthus dalmaticus, *E. graminifolius* and *E. serbicus* are all rather taller plants, with clusters of upright bells at the top of each flower stem, which do well in sunny well-drained conditions.

The wahlenbergias usually have quite large solitary flowers dancing in the wind on thin stems, above loose mats of narrow leaves. Most come from New Zealand, with a few from Australia and South Africa. The only one that seems reliably hardy in my garden is *W. albo-marginata*. It makes a carpet of tiny leaves with 2–3 in (5–8 cm) flower stems carrying single rather open bells, which vary in different forms from white to deep lavender blue. It has proved a good perennial, which flourishes between paving stones or in the open garden. The largest, *W. undulata* from South Africa, with very pale lilac-coloured flowers on 8 in (20 cm) stems, has surprised me by appearing in unexpected places where it has seeded itself gently around. Several other species of intermediate size are sometimes obtainable and it is easy to keep raising them from seed for the open garden, but they are only really perennial in the alpine house.

ERODIUM

This is a fascinating genus allied to *Geranium*, with several excellent easily-grown species. The smaller ones are most suitable for the rock garden, and there are one or two larger-growing species for the front of the border.

Most erodiums are attractive at all seasons, with fernlike silvery leaves. In fact, the easiest of them all, *Erodium chrysanthum*, produces its cream-coloured flowers so sparsely in many gardens, including my own, that it can be looked upon as a worthwhile foliage plant with an occasional bonus of flowers. In contrast to this, the easiest of the real dwarfs, *E. chamaedrioides*, smothers itself with almost stemless deep rose flowers above a low mat of small deep green rounded leaves. *E. reichardii* and *E. corsicum* are similar but a little larger in all their parts. *E. chamaedrioides* also has an attractive double-flowered form and a white form, usually with the faintest perceptible tinge of pink. Flowering of these begins during June and continues through the summer. At the time of writing this, in November, one plant is still in full flower!

There is a group of somewhat similar species which makes a mound 2–3 in (5–8 cm) high of very beautiful silver ferny leaves, with 4–6 in (10–15 cm) stems of flowers, generally white to pinkish in colour with a dark spot at the base of each petal and a delicate pencilling of the petals with darker lines. *E. macradenum* (*E. petraeum glandulosum*), *E. petraeum*, *E. guttatum* and *E. rupestre* all come into this group, and I suspect there has been hybridisation between them and some confusion in their names. All of them make good plants for the rock garden or raised bed, but are rather small for the mixed border.

Two bigger species are worth mentioning, even if not strictly alpines, as they associate well with shrubs and larger perennials. These are *E. carvifolium* and *E. manescavii*, both with fernlike green leaves up to a foot long and tall sprays

Figure 11   Erodium reichardii

of deep reddish-purple flowers, rather paler in *E. carvifolium*. I notice that these two are flowering well in November also!

E. *pelargonifolium* has rather coarse greyish-green leaves and pale pink flowers and seeds itself too freely for any but the wilder parts of the garden.

HELICHRYSUM

This is another large genus displaying an amazing range of sizes and shapes even among the species small enough to be included here.

There are several species which make low mats of silver leaves and only attain an inch or two even when in flower. Although some of them may be on the borderline of hardiness, I find that in scree conditions *Helichrysum bellidioides* and *H. milfordiae* (*H. marginatum*) are quite reliable. *H. belli-dioides* has small silver leaves along prostrate stems with tiny white everlasting flowers on short stems above them. *H. milfordiae* is a most beautiful plant with intensely hairy, almost white rosettes up to one inch (2.5 cm) across, which build up into a flat carpet and carry a few almost stemless comparatively large rose-pink flowers. It is not always as free flowering as one might wish, but is a striking low silver foliage plant for the foreground of the rock garden, easier to grow than its woolly appearance might suggest.

Some of the very hairy species need glass protection in the winter, but I have found *H. orientale* surprisingly tough in the open garden until our worst winter with 0°F temperature. It forms a mound up to 8 in (20 cm) high of grey, almost white, felted rosettes, above which rise 6 in (15 cm) stems with flat heads of several small yellow 'everlastings'. *H. virgineum* is very similar in growth, but has beautiful pink flowers and has never been very successful with me except in the alpine house.

H. selago is a fascinating foliage plant, with narrow whipcord stems that give the impression of being striped alternately with green and white. The flowers are insignificant but, as with most helichrysums, the foliage alone makes it worth growing, and it is quite easy in the rock garden. *H. coralloides*, another New Zealander like *H. selago*, is even more striking, its woolly stems thicker and more upright, with a similar striking striped appearance. It is one of the most spectacular alpine-house foliage plants, but I have succeeded outside with it for several years in a raised scree bed.

Helichrysum (Ozothamnus) ledifolium can become too large for a small rock garden, but it is so striking and slow-growing that I cannot resist recommending it as one of the best of all foliage plants of medium size. It makes a rather upright shrub with tiny deep green leaves with golden backs which catch the eye at all times, the golden-green appearance maintained throughout summer and winter. At midsummer its beauty is enhanced by the appearance of masses of reddish buds which open to inconspicuous white fluffy flowers. This shrub is remarkably hardy and only suffered badly when the temperature in my garden dropped to 0°F – a rare occurrence in the South of England.

Many more species will be found in catalogues, usually with excellent foliage but often failing to survive the average winter without protection. If in doubt, it is always worth giving them a trial in sunny scree conditions and rooting cuttings in case they fail.

IRIS
This is such a large and complicated genus that it is difficult to do it justice in a few paragraphs. The enthusiast is well-served by some excellent books on the genus, and here I will be very selective with a personal choice of some of my favourite smaller species. For the alpine enthusiast the bulbous species are perhaps the most important, but these are early-flowering and have been mentioned briefly at the beginning of this chapter.

There are several beautiful woodland species which will be described later with other shade-lovers. The mainly dwarf sun-loving species and hybrids which flower in the garden from May onwards come in a wide range of colours and sizes. They are nearly all easily grown and most will tolerate a limy soil. I grow the smallest of them in the rock garden, and use the larger plants for the sunny edges of mixed borders.

The small bearded irises are a complicated group found under a variety of names in catalogues. One name to look out for is *Iris attica*, once considered a subspecies of *Iris pumila*, but now a species in its own right. These are very small plants, possibly a little tender, in a wide range of colours from dark blue, through yellow to creamy-white, needing a sunny well-drained position in the garden, or alternatively in the alpine house. *Iris lutescens* is a very easily grown plant 6–12 in (15–30 cm) high in a wide variety of colours and flowering in May. *Iris pumila* and *Iris suaveolens* (*I. mellita*) are similar. I find that they look beautiful along the front of the border for a year or two but then they need splitting and replanting, because they start dying in the centre and flowering less freely, or else they become overrun with grass and other weeds.

One of the most beautiful groups of small iris comes from California and other western states in the USA, but unlike most species they need a neutral to acid soil, and enjoy plenty of humus. Gardening in one of the hotter counties, I find they do best in partial shade and must be kept reasonably moist in summer; further north they will flourish in full sun. *Iris innominata* is my favourite of these, with clumps of quite narrow leaves generally 4–8 in (10–20 cm) long and plenty of beautiful flowers on 8 in (20 cm) stems, most commonly in shades of yellow from pale cream to deep gold, but occasionally blue. Once planted, I like to leave them undisturbed, as they go from strength to strength for several years, unlike the species mentioned in the previous paragraph. *Iris douglasiana* is even easier to grow, but I find it a rather coarse plant which is not so generous with its flowers, usually in shades of lilac blue.

Iris tenax and *I. hartwegii* also belong here and are quite easy to grow in the same conditions. *Iris prismatica* is similar but rather tall. All are variable in colour and may appear in shades of cream to yellow or in shades of blue.

Iris unguicularis (*I. stylosa*) is well-known to most gardeners in its various colours from white through palest lavender to deep purple. It flowers through the winter in the hottest, driest place available. I love its flowers for cutting from November onwards but as a garden plant I resent its perpetually messy half-dead foliage. However, there are dwarf forms originating from Greece, usually under the name *I. cretensis*, in which the leaves are shorter and narrower and the flowers almost as large, but not always as freely produced.

Several other 'odds and ends' are worth mentioning. *Iris kerneriana* is a delightful species 12 in (30 cm) high, with abundant yellow flowers in June. *I. ruthenica* can be a little tall but varies in this respect and is very easy to grow, having deep lavender standards and pale falls with dark stripes. Its only fault is that it sometimes hides its flowers among the leaves.

Iris tectorum is a most beautiful Chinese species, usually 10–14 in (25–35 cm) high, with very large flat-topped flowers, the standards standing out horizontally. The usual colour is lavender blue with darker veining, but there is also an exquisite white variety. *Iris setosa*, from Japan and North America, is very variable in height from a dwarf of 6 in (15 cm) up to 18 in (45 cm). The flower stems usually carry two or three blooms, which are large with small pointed standards, and vary somewhat in their shade of lilac-blue with darker veining. As in *I. tectorum* there is a good white form. Both these species do best in a sunny site and are excellent growing on the sunny side of a mixed border.

LEUCANTHEMUM

This small genus allied closely to *Chrysanthemum* is well worth mentioning for one plant alone, *Leucanthemum (Chrysanthemum) hosmariense*, one of the most satisfactory medium-sized alpines both for foliage and flower. It makes a mound of glistening silver finely-cut leaves, remaining in good condition throughout the year. Apart from its beauty as a foliage plant I find it has one of the longest flowering seasons, rarely being without one or two of its large white daisies with central yellow eyes.

The only other reasonably hardy species that is readily obtainable is *Leucanthemum catananche*, which makes a spreading mat of finely-cut green leaves surrounded in May or June by delicate pale orange dark-eyed daisies. It sulks in heavy soil, but I find it needs watching in more suitable well-drained conditions as it can spread sideways sufficiently to overlay smaller plants.

LEWISIA

This is a favourite genus of all alpine enthusiasts. Many of the species are quite easy to grow in appropriate conditions, but some require special treatment under glass. All reward the grower with a stunning display of flowers for several weeks on end.

Although there are numerous species growing wild in the mountains of the USA, some of them have interbred so much in cultivation that it is difficult to obtain the true plants, and their places have been taken by seed strains. This may worry the purist, but the average gardener can delight in the strains available. These are usually found either under clonal names with no species specified, or as subspecies and varieties of *Lewisia cotyledon*. All of them will have similar rosettes of succulent leaves up to 9 in (22 cm) across, building up gradually into large mounds. The flowering stems rise well above the leaves and carry sprays of several flowers in shades of pink, or less commonly white, orange or purple.

Perhaps the ideal way to grow these lewisias, with the exception of the few needing a drying-off period in summer, is in a retaining wall with rich, well-drained soil behind it.

Many years ago I saw lewisias at their best. I was visiting the famous gardens at Bodnant when I came across a retaining wall some four feet high, which had been planted with *Lewisia cotyledon* in every available crack. The result, when I was there in early summer, was an amazing sheet of pink flowers visible from afar. I have never seen them so spectacular elsewhere, but I am convinced that this is the best way to grow the easier species. Planted on their sides, there is less danger of excessive wet in winter rotting their crowns. In practice many of them will thrive on the flat as long as the drainage is very good. They seem to grow better in damp climates in full exposure, and in the warmer counties are probably best facing north, or at least west or east, rather than south.

The largest and most striking species is *Lewisia tweedyi*, but it needs special care, as the crowns of older plants tend to rot after flowering unless the plant is kept almost bone dry around the neck at that time. The flowers usually are pale

Figure 12   Lewisia columbiana

peach in colour, but they can be white or deep rose. I would put it high on any list of plants for the alpine house, only demanding extra care with watering. More extreme treatment is needed for the exquisite *Lewisia rediviva*, which has a small rosette of short narrow succulent leaves and huge flowers of satiny-pink or white. It forms a carrot-like root, which has to be dried off completely after flowering and started gently into growth with a little water from below in autumn – alas, not a plant for the open garden, but still among my favourite alpines, especially after seeing it grow in the Nevada desert, where the poor stony ground became sheeted with its pink flowers in June. *Lewisia brachycalyx* is somewhat similar with large white or pale pink flowers, requiring the same treatment. *L. pygmaea* and its subspecies *longipetala*, the former with small pink flowers, the latter with white flowers and reddish stamens, are easy to grow and indeed are worth trying in the garden. I have kept *L. longipetala* for several seasons outside in the scree, although it never flowers as abundantly as under glass.

There are several other smaller species that are excellent in the rock garden, notably *Lewisia columbiana* and its varieties, which have much smaller more compact rosettes and sprays of flowers 4–6 in (10–15 cm) long, varying from pale pink to deep magenta. I have found these long-lived in scree conditions even on the flat.

LINUM

These are mainly easy sun-loving plants, some of them a little tall for the small rock garden, with a few rare and tricky species for the alpine house. Two excellent smaller alpines are *Linum* 'Gemmell's Hybrid' and *Linum salsoloides* 'Nanum'. The former is a semi-shrubby plant slowly attaining 8–10 in (20–25 cm) with glaucous leaves and large yellow flowers during May and June. The latter is very different, making a slow-growing mat of tiny leaves with comparatively large white flowers, the whole plant only an inch or two high; it looks delicate but has proved an excellent long-lived perennial in a raised bed in my garden.

Linum arboreum and *L. flavum* are yellow-flowered shrubs 12–18 in (30–45 cm) high, for the large rock garden or among taller plants in the border. Although yellow is the predominant colour of the genus there are two good tall species with slender stems and sprays of blue flowers over a long period, *L. perenne* and *L. narbonnense*. Although they are rather tall – up to 2 ft (60 cm) in flower – they are so delicate and graceful that it seems appropriate to include them among alpines. They are reasonably self-supporting, but I like to place them between shrubs of medium size. Here, their pale blue flowers combine well with some of the pink and white cistus species and, like these, they have a long flowering season. They can seed themselves around freely but are quite easy to extract where they are unwanted.

MERTENSIA

Most of the species 'sell on sight' when seen growing in pots, with their beautiful leaves and small hanging blue bell-shaped flowers, but they are not all easy to grow and the requirements of different species seem to vary.

The most unusual and spectacular are *M. maritima*, our native oyster plant, and its subspecies *M. asiatica*, which seems very similar but is a little easier to grow, in my experience. They both make clumps of remarkable pale blue rounded leaves from which arise semi-prostrate stems with sprays of small pale blue bells. Unfortunately they do not like normal garden conditions and I have found them most successful in deep scree, where they can be left undisturbed and will probably provide a nice crop of self-sown seedlings to take the place of any old plants that die. They do, unfortunately!

Mertensia virginica is the commonest and easiest species, which grows well in partial shade with plenty of humus. In good conditions it may grow up to 2 ft (60 cm), but is frequently less. It has slender stems with narrow blue-green leaves and sprays of small blue flowers in spring. It dies down rapidly after planting, so care must be taken to mark its position. I find it only too easy to dig it up when planting something else later! *Mertensia pterocarpa* is a more satisfactory and more 'alpine' plant with beautiful broad glaucous leaves and 8–10 in (20–25 cm) spikes of typical blue flowers. Even smaller is *M. echioides*, in which the flowers are only 6 in (15 cm) high.

6. *Roscoea cautleoides* (sun-loving/mid-season)

7. *Campanula haylodgensis* 'Warley White' (sun-loving/mid-season)

8. *Mertensia maritima* (sun-loving/mid-season)

9. *Linum salsoloides Nanum* (sun-loving/mid-season)

10. *Aquilegia flabellata* (sun-loving/mid-season)

11. *Zauschneria* 'Glasnevin' (sun-loving/late season)

12. *Cyclamen hederifolium* (shade-loving/late season)

13. *Ranunculus ficaria* 'Brazen Hussy' (shade-loving/early season)

ORIGANUM

The introduction of one or two new dwarf species from Turkey and the appearance of hybrids from them seems to have stimulated interest in a genus mainly valued previously for culinary purposes.

The two exciting introductions or, more correctly, one introduction and one re-introduction are *Origanum rotundifolium* and *O. amanum*. *O. amanum* was introduced soon after the last war and found to be an excellent alpine-house plant. It makes a low mat an inch or two high, above which in August arise hop-like rounded heads of pink-flushed bracts, from which appear long narrow pink flowers. It was never looked upon as a satisfactory garden plant until the re-introduction some fifteen years ago of a hardier form, which in my own garden has survived some terrible winters. It was introduced at the same time as *O. rotundifolium*, which is very similar in its low growth but becomes completely hidden in hop-like clusters of delicate pale green bracts, among which the flowers are almost invisible. For any lover of green flowers this is a delight and must be one of the finest alpine introductions of recent years. Given a well-drained sunny position this has proved at least as hardy as *O. amanum*, both plants having survived temperatures of 0°F in my own garden. A white form of *O. amanum* has recently become available, which should prove a splendid addition to the late summer flowering alpines. Even more beautiful are two hybrids of *O. rotundifolium*, which appeared accidentally in different gardens a few years ago, and are among the choicest plants for the rock garden or scree. These are 'Kent Beauty' and 'Barbara Tingey'. They are very similar in growth to their parent, but the heads of bracts gradually take on an ever-increasing pink flush in the course of several weeks. 'Kent Beauty' is perhaps the most spectacular, but in my experience it is less soundly perennial and a little earlier flowering than 'Barbara Tingey', so that it is undoubtedly worth growing them both to provide colour when good flowering alpines are becoming few and far between.

There are several taller species, notably *O. laevigatum* and *O. tournefortii*, with upright stems and sprays of small deep pink flowers, darkest purple in *O. laevigatum* 'Hopley's Form'. These are a little tall for the rock garden but are excellent associated with silver foliage plants and other perennials towards the front of a border.

O. dictamnus is marvellous with some winter protection, making a mound of heavily-felted silver-grey leaves and typical dark purple origanum flowers from dark-flushed bracts.

OXALIS

Although more likely to provoke a shudder than any great feelings of pleasure, this genus in fact contains some of the most excellent trouble-free dwarf plants, as well as some diabolical weeds!

The two most satisfactory species are probably *Oxalis adenophylla* and *O. enneaphylla*. Both make a gradually spreading tangle of curious scaly rhizomes just below the soil surface, from which the beautiful grey trifoliate leaves unfurl in spring, to be followed by large round wide-open flowers, generally in shades of pink, during early summer. *O. adenophylla* is largest in all its parts and the flowers are deep pink. *O. enneaphylla* has many named varieties, varying in colour and compactness. *O. enneaphylla* var. *minutifolia* is, as the name implies, very small-growing with short flowering stems. *O. enneaphylla* var. *rosea* and var. *rubra* have darker flowers, and there is also a form *alba*. None of these ever becomes troublesome – in fact, my only wish is that they would increase more quickly!

Hybrids have been raised between *O. enneaphylla* and *O. laciniata*, the latter a much more difficult species, with flowers of very dark blue with even darker veining and tiny grey leaves, which struggles along in rich scree with some shade in my garden. The hybrid 'Ione Hecker' has many of its virtues and none of its faults, in fact it is as easy as *O. enneaphylla*; it has very large lavender flowers with dark purple veining, sometimes appearing almost as dark as *O. laciniata*. This is one of the best recent introductions to the alpine world.

O. lobata is a tiny species for the rock garden. It has the curious habit of producing pale green leaves in the spring, which rapidly die down again to the alarm of the poor grower. They then reappear in the autumn accompanied by delightful small yellow oxalis flowers. Two other species worth looking out for are *O. inops* and *O. obtusa*, both very low-growing with greyish leaves and pink flowers.

PAPAVER

Miniature poppies are among my favourite alpines, and there are several species that, though generally short-lived, will seed themselves around the rock garden, or in the front of a sunny border. *Papaver alpinum* itself is most commonly a delicate shade of pale pink. Although individual plants may not survive more than a year or two, it seeds itself around gently and, if kept away from other forms and other species generally, keeps its delicious colour. There is also a white form, similar to or maybe identical with *P. burseri*, which is sometimes available from seed lists. These all grow about 6 in (15 cm) high in flower, with dainty tufts of deeply cut hairy leaves.

The same effect may be obtained in yellow, with a choice of several very similar species. The most satisfactory here seems to be the Japanese *P. faurei* (most commonly offered as *P. miyabeanum*), a better perennial than *P. alpinum* with pale greenish-yellow flowers on 6 in (15 cm) stems. *P. rhaeticum* and *P. kerneri* are closely allied to *P. alpinum* and are very similar with their attractive hairy leaves and yellow flowers. They are all astonishingly beautiful and yet not often seen in gardens, maybe because they do not make good 'nurseryman's plants' in pots. Grow them from seed!

PENSTEMON

Many of the easiest penstemons have been described already as carpeting plants. In addition there are several equally easily grown species of more shrubby habit. Perhaps the best of these is *Penstemon pinifolius* – a small shrub with tiny needle-like pale green leaves and brilliant orange-red narrow flowers in early summer. An exciting variety of it, possibly a sport, is now becoming available, *P. pinifolius* 'Mersea Yellow', identical except in its pale yellow colour.

Penstemon rupicola also makes a low-growing shrub but has quite broad deep green leaves and deep rose flowers, except in its pure white form. The names *P. davidsonii*, *P. menziesii*, *P. newberryi* and *P. roezlii* all cover a range of similar shrubby plants, generally 6–12 in (15–30 cm) high with typical long tubular flowers in shades of pink, red or purple. The names are somewhat muddled, so you must rely on the catalogue descriptions or their appearance in flower when choosing your plants! They should all be quite easy as long as you choose a sunny position and well-drained soil. *P. rupicola* and *P. davidsonii* are the nearest to red, and the form of *P. roezlii* generally available also has flowers of this colour. The true *P. roezlii*, and also *P. menziesii*, should have deep purple flowers, a colour always found in the similar 'Six Hills Hybrid'.

PRIMULA
Many of the best alpine primulas have been described under early-flowering alpines; others will be discussed with shade-lovers. The only common mid-season primulas are the Asiatic candelabra species, which generally come into their own in May, and will be considered later with other shade-loving plants. It is worth mentioning here that most of them will thrive in northern counties in sunny conditions as long as there is plenty of moisture-retaining humus in the soil, but occasional watering may be needed during dry spells.

RAOULIA
These are carpeting plants par excellence, but can be a little tricky and certainly are too small for mixed planting in the border, as they form little more than a film on the surface of the soil. In the rock garden they look very attractive, and can be used as cover for bulbs. The most straightforward are *Raoulia australis*, a carpet of glistening silver, *R. lutescens* and *R. subsericea*, similar or identical film-like pale green mats, which turn to bright yellow as the flowers open, and *R. glabra*, which makes a green carpet with tiny white flowers.

In addition to these there are several difficult cushion plants for the alpine house, such as *R. eximia* and *R. grandiflora*, which will challenge the expert.

ROSCOEA
It seems surprising that roscoeas are not seen more often in gardens, as they are easily grown and yet look remarkably exotic, with large orchid-like flowers with a prominent lower lip and an upstanding hooded upper petal. They seem to do best in partial shade in the south, but given a reasonable amount of moisture and plenty of humus they should thrive in the open elsewhere.

The nomenclature of the purple-flowered species is somewhat confused, but there is no doubt about the excellent yellow-flowered species *Roscoea cautleoides*, a splendid plant 8–10 in (20–25 cm) high with pale cream-coloured flowers in June. The 'Kew' form has larger flowers with broader petals and

Figure 13   Sisyrinchium douglasii

seems to me to be paler in colour. I think the two plants sufficiently distinct to make them both worth growing – flower size is not everything.

There are several similar plants with sumptuous deepest purple flowers, the commonest being *R. auriculata*, often available as *R. purpurea*, and *R. purpurea* itself (often listed as *R. procera*), with paler and larger flowers. These generally open only one flower to a stem at one time, whereas the similarly coloured *R. humeana* has a cluster of flowers opening together. *R. alpina* is similar in colour but considerably smaller. *R.* 'Beesiana' is sometimes offered, probably a hybrid, with pale yellow flowers streaked with purple.

The roscoeas make very leafy plants when not in flower and I prefer to grow them among shrubs or in the front of a border, rather than with smaller plants in the rock garden where their lushness seems somewhat out of place.

SISYRINCHIUM
Apart from the beautiful early-flowering *S. douglasii* with its large nodding purple bells, the best of the genus are sun-loving and summer-flowering. There are many weeds among them – weeds because they self-sow to excess – but the

following can be relied upon to behave themselves! *S. macounii* var. *alba* has become widely grown and is an excellent dwarf plant, making a clump of iris-like leaves 3 in (8 cm) long, with a long succession of large white flowers. It is easy to grow anywhere and exceptionally easy to propagate by division. This is its commonest name, although there is some doubt whether it is in fact *S. idahoense* var. *alba* or *S. bellum* var. *alba*. *S. macounii* itself is not often seen, but *S. bellum* is a very similar if not identical plant with good blue flowers. *S. californica* has quite large yellow flowers, but I find that it sows itself a little too freely. The same applies to *Sisyrinchium* 'Biscutella', the small flowers of which are a strange dusky mixture of brown, yellow and purple, which is rapidly taking over a patch of my rock garden with its seedlings.

Sisyrinchium filifolium is a beautiful slender plant with narrow leaves and stems to about 8 in (20 cm), each with one or two large white flowers heavily veined with brownish-purple. This needs well-drained conditions and is very slow to make a sizeable clump, which is sad because it is one of the most beautiful of all the species.

VERBASCUM

This is not only a genus of statuesque plants for the middle or back of the border. It contains several desirable species small enough to consider here, with a warning that the best of them resent excessive winter wet. This particularly applies to the beautiful species *Verbascum dumulosum* and *V. pestallozae*, with heavily felted grey-green leaves and spikes of yellow flowers. They are the easiest possible cold-house plants, making a mound of leaves a foot across and not quite so high, smothered in flowers in May and June. In the open garden they do best in scree conditions, but tend only to survive the winter when planted on their sides in a retaining wall, so that the rain does not linger in their woolly rosettes. I have even seen them surviving winters in Aviemore in Scotland, planted in that way.

Verbascum spinosum is similar in having woolly grey leaves and in resenting winter wet, but the leaves are small and the whole plant is spiny. Its hybrid 'Letitia' resembles it but is an easier plant for the open garden, producing its yellow brown-eyed flowers over a long period in summer. *V. wiedmanniana* is occasionally offered in the trade, with a flat rosette of dark green leaves from which arise 12–18 in (30–45 cm) spikes of rich deep purple flowers. It is not long-lived, but it seeds around very freely and only comes true if there are no other verbascums nearby. Otherwise it produces a range of colours between yellow and purple, many of them quite attractive, but sometimes the plants are too tall. Recently the true *V. wiedmanniana* has been introduced with grey hairy rosettes.

Mid-season Shrubs
In describing some of the easiest of alpine plants with sufficient impact to make them suitable for association with larger plants as well as in the rock garden, I have so far omitted many of the obviously shrubby genera which can be used

effectively in the same way, such obvious choices as the dwarf brooms and willows, the helianthemums, and the daphnes – often considered the elite of alpine shrubs.

With limited space, I am omitting the vast range of dwarf conifers, which seem to be becoming increasingly popular, especially planted in conjunction with heathers. Although this combination is labour-saving and must presumably appeal to many gardeners, I do not feel it comes within the scope of a book on alpine plants. On the other hand, there is certainly a place for truly dwarf conifers as accent plants in the rock garden, whether you use the little upright spires of *Juniperus communis* 'Compressa', or the tight buns of various *Chamaecyparis obtusa* forms. The choice is endless. See them at a nursery or in other gardens, and study carefully and critically any information about their height and width after ten years of growth. Many so-called dwarfs will be taller than their owners after twenty or thirty years!

BROOMS

Under this heading I include the various low-growing species of *Genista*, *Cytisus*, *Chamaecytisus* and *Chamaespartium*. They are all easily grown, generally yellow-flowerd plants, which will flourish in light soils in full sun. They vary in size from tiny ground-hugging mats upwards, and several of the larger species are really only suitable for the largest rock garden, or better still for the foreground of a mixed or shrub border. They look particularly good in association with blues – for example, in front of ceanothus, or combined with the forms of *Lithodora diffusa*. One of the best of these large species is *Cytisus kewensis* with masses of pale cream flowers on a wide-spreading shrub, which may mound up to 2 ft (60 cm) or more eventually. *Cytisus* × *beanii* is of similar height but is more compact and has deep yellow flowers. *Genista lydia* is similar in colour but has arching stems, giving it a particularly graceful habit. *Chamaecytisus purpureus* (*Cytisus purpureus*) also makes a spreading mound of semi-prostrate branches, eventually 1–2 ft (30–60 cm) high, with rosy-purple flowers in May. It has a very attractive albino form, which I rarely see in other gardens.

Several species are small enough to associate with alpine plants in the rock garden. *Genista pilosa*, preferably in its most prostrate form 'Procumbens', makes a flat carpet of prostrate stems, never more than 6 in (15 cm) high, but capable of spreading eventually to several feet, killing everything beneath it. Watch its neighbours! The abundant small deep-yellow flowers appear, as in almost all the brooms, in early to mid summer. *Cytisus ardoinii* is a little taller with hairy leaves, and only spreads slowly – this is one of my favourite dwarf species. Perhaps the most exciting is *C. demissus* (*C. demissus* var. *hirsutus*), which needs a very well-drained sunny spot to do well. It is a low prostrate woolly-leaved plant with exceptionally large yellow flowers with reddish-brown keels. I grow it on top of a low sunny wall where it can hang down over the face. *Genista villarsii* is another tiny species needing special care. It only grows an inch or two high and forms a cluster of thin grey stems with very small leaves and deep yellow flowers.

Chamaespartium sagittalis (*Genista sagittalis*) is an unusual broom in having stems flattened into thin wings, tending to turn upright at their tips and rarely more than 6–8 in (15–20 cm) high. In a hot sunny position it produces a sprinkling of deep yellow flowers in June. I have never found it very free-flowering, but that is probably because it has become overshadowed by trees over the years.

SALIX

There are a surprising number of dwarf willows suitable for the rock garden. Many of them, like the brooms, spread sideways a long way and need careful positioning so that they cannot swamp more delicate plants. Few of the willows could be described as spectacular, but some have very attractive catkins and most have interesting foliage. Here are a few suggestions.

Salix × boydii is a fascinating slow-growing miniature, small enough for a permanent position in a trough. It has an upright gnarled appearance with rounded woolly grey leaves and occasional nondescript catkins – a real plant of character. *Salix reticulata* is another species worth growing for its leaves and habit alone. It is prostrate with large rounded heavily-veined green leaves, and spreads quite slowly. *Salix retusa*, *S. myrtilloides* and *S. serpyllifolia* are equally prostrate with tiny glossy leaves and small upright catkins in spring.

In contrast to these, *Salix lanata* is too big for the rock garden but is a dramatic low shrub, with intensely hairy grey leaves and large grey catkins that become yellow as their pollen develops. *S. apoda* has similar growth and similar dramatic catkins, but the leaves are green.

None of these willows requires wet conditions, but they will all tolerate heavy soil without much added drainage. In lighter soils the addition of plenty of humus should suit them, and they will grow in full sun or light shade.

HELIANTHEMUM

Most of the rock roses are low-growing shrubs with a mass of flowers during the summer, in a huge range of colours from white, through yellows, pinks and deep reds. They are all worth growing, and flourish in the hottest possible place in full sun, preferably in light well-drained soil. Some have quite attractive grey leaves, but the generally hot colours are the main attraction and I think they look best grown together in mixed colours, rather than associated with more delicate alpines. Alternatively, they can be grown in patches of one suitable colour in the front of a shrub border.

One of the most effective plantings of rock roses that I have seen was in a neighbour's garden, where they had been planted in gaps in a broad crazy paving path, using a galaxy of mixed colours. They had grown so splendidly that the path had largely disappeared, but in the height of summer there was an amazing sea of colour between two stretches of lawn.

Among the dozens of varieties available one which particularly appeals to me is 'Boughton double Primrose'. This has very dark green leaves and plentiful double flowers in a pleasant shade of pale primrose, very different

Figure 14   Daphne petraea

from the hot colours of the majority. One species also is worthy of note because it deserves a place among the true alpines. This is *H. lunulatum*, a neat little compact grey-leaved shrub, with small yellow flowers for a long period around midsummer.

DAPHNE

Why is this genus so popular? Daphnes are almost all shrubs with pink to purple or white beautifully scented flowers, varying in height from an inch or two to two or three feet. They certainly do not flaunt their charms, but they all have an irresistible quiet beauty; in addition, many of them present a challenge, with a tendency to die suddenly and unexpectedly, completely or in large patches. On the whole they seem to like a rich but well-drained soil, and the species mentioned here should thrive in a sunny or lightly shaded position and will take many years to achieve more than 2 ft (60 cm) in height.

The smallest and most sought-after is *Daphne petraea* 'Grandiflora', an extremely slow-growing shrublet with deep pink clusters of scented flowers in May. Although usually cosseted in the alpine house, it can be grown outside in scree conditions, or in a trough, or planted in tufa. *Daphne arbuscula* is another beautiful compact shrub with larger green leaves, which I find easier to grow in the rock garden. It is a most desirable dwarf with deep-rose scented flowers. *D. oleoides* is almost as compact, with small grey-green leaves and masses of white flowers followed by orange fruits. This has a totally undeserved reputation for tenderness. I have grown it for years from seed collected in Turkey and it has flourished in a trough and in the open garden, in spite of our bad winters.

Perhaps the best daphne for general garden use is *D. cneorum* or its form *eximium*, which can make a low-spreading shrub a foot or two across but rarely more than 10–12 in (25–30 cm) high, with wonderfully scented pink flowers. It has a trickier dwarf form, *D. cneorum* var. *pygmaeum*, needing similar treatment to *D. petraea*. *D. blagayana* also has a spreading habit, its branches rooting as they go and becoming very sparsely furnished with leaves in the middle, unless they are constantly top-dressed. It tends in fact to be an untidy straggler (with me!), but has fine clusters of white scented flowers in April, which make even its wretched growth habit worthwhile.

Daphne has several compact shrubby species, taller than those already mentioned but unlikely to outgrow their space in the rock garden. *Daphne collina* and *D. sericea* are very similar, making a round dome of evergreen leaves with clusters of small pinkish-lilac flowers in May, increasing in height by an inch or two a year. *D. retusa* has larger leaves and is almost equally slow-growing, whereas *D. tangutica*, though similar in its early stages, will be taller and looser-growing eventually.

The yellow species of medium height most likely to be encountered are *D. giraldii*, which tends with me to flower and fruit itself to death, and *D. jezoensis* and *D. kamschatcensis*, closely allied plants with the disconcerting habit of shedding their leaves for a period in the summer.

There are several other hybrids and species, all well worth growing. Try to propagate them from seed (if any) or cuttings, as they all seem to share this tendency to a short life!

OTHER SHRUBS

Apart from the major genera there are one or two odds and ends. *Leptospermum* is a genus of very attractive shrubs from Australasia, many of which are far too large and too tender for inclusion, but the few dwarf varieties, mainly forms of *L. scoparium*, are excellent plants for the cold greenhouse or alpine house, or even for sheltered gardens. They make hummocks of tiny needle-like leaves, usually tinged with silver or bronze, and have masses of comparatively large flowers in shades from white to deep reddish-purple. Every time I admire them in flower I wish they were hardy enough to be good perennials outside. Alas, you must live in the south-west of England for that pleasure!

Petrophytum is a genus worth looking out for. Closely allied to *Spiraea*, they all have neat upright spikes of white flowers above compact rosettes of leaves, which are ground-hugging in *P. caespitosum* and the slightly larger *P. cinerascens*, and make a neat very slow-growing 'bun' in *P. hendersonii*.

The easiest thymes have been described (see p. 37), but one or two of the best are shrubby in habit and too tender for any but sheltered gardens. The best and commonest is *Thymus membranaceus*, quite a slow-growing shrub with exceptionally large heads of good white flowers. The large-flowered pink *T. longiflorus* and *T. cilicius* are occasionally offered.

Mainly under Glass

While considering mid-season alpines I have mentioned several which need some protection, but whereas there are several early-flowering genera such as *Androsace* and *Dionysia* in which the majority need this care, there are far fewer that flower in summer.

The eriogonums – the buckwheats – are an interesting North American genus, usually with silver-grey foliage, varying enormously in their shapes and sizes but all worth growing with some protection from winter wet. I keep trying them in the garden, but there is only one which I have found entirely satisfactory – *Eriogonum torreyanum*, which makes an 8 in (20 cm) high shrub with green leaves and an abundance of deep yellow fluffy flowers in June.

Another North American genus, *Townsendia*, contains the elite of Compositae for the alpine house, but they are short-lived in the open, even in scree conditions. All are low-growing mats or buns with exceptionally large daisy flowers in shades usually of lavender or white. *T. formosa* is probably the easiest of them outside.

There have been recent introductions of seed of *Acantholimum* species, and these are well worth trying in the hottest and best-drained site possible on the rock garden. They make tight, extremely spiny buns, attractive throughout the year, with spikes of pink flowers during the early summer, not always freely produced in our climate. *A. glumaceum* has been around for a long time and is easily grown given the conditions specified above. *A. venustum* is now becoming common and is a superior plant, but more exacting in its requirements for sun and good drainage. Any of the other species are worth trying.

Late Season

The size of the last section was an indication of the abundance of alpines which flower between May and July, when they compete with so many shrubs and other perennials. In late summer and autumn the shrub season is virtually over until the onset of autumn colour and fruit, but colour in the garden can be maintained by skilful use of perennials well into September.

From September onwards bulbs come back into their own with *Agapanthus*, *Nerine* and *Schizostylis* among the larger background plants and *Colchicum*, autumn-flowering *Crocus* and *Cyclamen* among the smaller plants for the front of the border or rock garden. With these dwarf bulbs, which are so important to give late colour in the rock garden, a few other alpine plants can be associated. Most of these can be classed among the easy carpeters; they represent several substantial genera with some 'odds and ends', and only gentians and erodiums among the typical alpines.

Easy Carpeters

Among those already described, the diascias and osteospermums especially go on and on continuously with a few blooms, and may have a second generous flush of flowering. Some geraniums also can be relied upon to have late flowers, for example 'Anne Folkard'. The asters and erigerons described earlier are also still flowering at this time.

SEMPERVIVUM

I have put sempervivums here because, although they can be effective at any season, they are more likely to appeal when flowers are few and far between. They are grown mainly for their foliage effect, but a few flowers usually appear during the summer months. There are a great many species and hybrids, all with beautiful rosettes in shades of green to purple, often with edging of a different colour, and, in the varieties of *S. arachnoideum*, covered with a network of fine hairs like spiders' webs. They can be used in various ways and I can think of several gardens where they have formed a marvellous coloured patchwork on level ground, in a sunny position in very well-drained soil. However, I feel that they are seen at their best when associated with rocks, either mingling with the rockwork of a rock garden, or planted in the interstices of a retaining rock wall of any height from two courses upwards. The smaller-rosetted species have a marvellous way of moulding themselves into the cracks and around the rocks with the minimum of care and attention. The choice is so wide that I make no suggestions. See them growing at a nursery and select those which appeal most.

SEDUM

Another vast genus, the majority of which flower during the later summer months. For reasons which are hard to analyse sedums are not very popular with alpine enthusiasts, and I grow few myself, but just as *Sedum spectabile* forms make a tremendous contribution to the autumn border, so there are several truly excellent late-flowering plants for the rock garden or elsewhere. They are all easy in full sun, so they can be used to prolong the season when planted along the edge of a sunny border with shrubs or perennials behind them.

There are not many purple-leaved plants among alpines and one of the best of these is *Sedum* 'Vera Jameson'. It has low arching stems of small succulent purple leaves, terminating in late summer in flat heads of deep red flowers, making a striking contrast to some of the low-growing silver-leaved artemisias.

Another striking foliage plant is the variegated form of *Sedum kamtschaticum* with upright stems of green and gold leaves and heads of deep yellow flowers. *Sedum hidakanum* is a reliable species with spreading stems of succulent bluish leaves, with the typical grape-like bloom of many sedums, and wide heads of small deep rose flowers. A very similar effect can be obtained from forms of *Sedum spathulifolium*, 'Purpureum' having purple leaves and 'Capa Blanca' bluish-white leaves, both with deep yellow flowers.

This is a very limited selection of some of the best non-invasive species of sedums. Nurseries specialising in them can offer a huge choice of others!

ZAUSCHNERIA

Although not very well-known, I think this is one of the best genera of alpines for late colour, and here in Kent most species have proved reliably hardy. Apart from an albino and an uncommon pink variety of *Zauschneria californica*, the colour is a vivid orange-red, which may not be easy to combine with other colours, but these alpines flower so late that this problem can be avoided and most of them have grey-green leaves, which are a good foil for the flowers. Accidents do happen and I have the vivid red *Zauschneria* 'Glasnevin' within screaming distance of the brilliant magenta *Senecio pulcher*. This combination should be studied by anyone who considers that flower colours cannot clash!

One authority has lumped all zauschnerias as *Epilobium canum*, but since I doubt whether this will be followed quickly by nurserymen I will retain the better-known names. The commonest species is *Zauschneria californica*, which forms a spreading shrub of up to a foot high, with grey-green leaves and narrow tubular bright red flowers for a long period in late summer. The most reliable in my garden is 'Glasnevin', sometimes called 'Dublin', a marvellous plant which has green leaves and a more spreading habit, and a remarkably long flowering season. *Z. cana* (*microphylla*) has very small grey leaves on an upright bush, and 'Benton End', occasionally available, seems to be a particularly good more silvery form of it.

GENTIANS

There can be little doubt that the autumn-flowering gentians are the elite of late-flowering alpines, but alas they can only be enjoyed by those gardeners with an acid soil, unless they can be grown in containers. Lime is death to most of them and measures to combat it in naturally alkaline conditions are probably a waste of energy. However, even in an alkaline soil you can enjoy *Gentiana septemfida*, which generally flowers in August. It is a leafier plant than the later-flowering species and the flowers in terminal clusters are smaller, but the colour is a good deep blue and the species is undoubtedly worth growing, especially if you cannot have *G. sino-ornata* and its allies. It is a pity that *G. farreri* has become rare, as it will apparently grow in spite of a moderate amount of lime. It is perhaps the most beautiful colour of all, an amazing pale Cambridge blue, and every time I see its electrifying colour I wish the plant were less temperamental. At present, with fingers crossed, I am growing it in a raised scree bed with extra leaf-mould and it seems happy.

The remaining gentians need acid soil with plenty of leaf-mould and peat and adequate moisture. If the soil is moist at all times they flower better in full sun, but my experience in Kent is that they are easier to grow in partial shade and flower quite well there. The classic autumn-flowering gentian is *G. sino-ornata*, which is very easy in the right soil and can be split up in the spring into individual thongs which rapidly become sizeable flowering plants for autumn. After a year or two they may exhaust the soil and it is best to split them regularly every two or three years, or more often if you are trying to build up a

Figure 15   Gentiana sino-ornata

large colony quickly. Replant in soil that has had fresh leaf-mould incorporated, unless you are lucky enough to have natural woodland for them. *G. sino-
ornata* has wonderful large dark blue trumpets in great abundance, which last
well in water if you pick them for the house. Over the years extensive
hybridisation of this and other gentians has been carried out, so that many
named strains and individual clones are available, in different shades of blue
and with differently shaped trumpets. Some of the main parents have been *G.
farreri*, *G. veitchiorum* (very dark blue) and *G. ornata* (with short tubby bells).
None of these is easy to grow, at least in the south, but all have contributed to
the modern easiest hybrids available. This is another genus where it is advisable
to see the plants in flower, either in a specialist nursery or exhibited at such
shows as Vincent Square or Harrogate, where magnificent displays can be seen
in autumn, or at Botanic Gardens such as Wisley, Kew, Harlow Car, Ness or
Edinburgh. Some of the most popular are 'Drakes Strain', 'Inshriach Hybrids',
× 'Macaulayi', 'Kingfisher', × *stevenagensis* and 'Susan Jane'.

Such glorious colours are to be found among the gentians that it seems
almost sacrilegious to consider white ones, but there are two which I think are
well worth growing, *G. sino-ornata* var. *alba* and 'Mary Lyle', the latter having
larger and more cream-coloured flowers. They make a striking contrast
growing among their blue counterparts, especially in the shade where the blues
may seem a little subdued.

Although it is generally too large for the rock garden, I cannot resist mentioning *Gentiana asclepediaea*, the willow gentian, as it is such an invaluable medium-sized plant which can be relied upon to flower well even in deep shade. I planted it originally in a peat bed beneath a north wall with its white variety, and I now find it appearing in various parts of the garden from self-sown seedlings, the plants equally divided between blue and white. My plants in this somewhat dry garden rarely attain more than 2 ft (60 cm), with spectacular foot long spires of small blue or white trumpets. In ideal conditions, especially in northern counties, it may well be as tall as three or four feet. An attractive named clone 'Knightshayes' is sometimes available, in which the blue trumpets have white markings in the throat.

Easy 'Odds and Ends'
Let us now look at a handful of excellent easy plants for the front of a border, which do not belong to major genera but are invaluable for providing some late colour.

The ceratostigmas, *C. willmottiae* and *C. plumbaginoides* are a little tall to be considered alpines, attaining 12–18 in (30–45 cm), but they are excellent for late colour with heads of deep blue flowers on upright stems, more spreading in *C. willmottiae*. As an added bonus the leaves take on reddish tints in autumn, when most of the late colour is at a higher level. They are robust enough to make an excellent foreground to large shrubs, including roses or azaleas, but they need a reasonable amount of sun to colour well.

Silene schafta is not spectacular, but is a reliable and easy plant with a long succession of deep rose flowers on 6 in (15 cm) stems from July onwards. Give it plenty of space in the rock garden or use it as a border edging. Recently a variety 'Shell Pink' has appeared with more beautiful soft pink flowers – certainly a plant to look out for.

Serratula seoanei (*S. shawii*) also has a long flowering period, similar to that of *Silene schafta*. It forms a clump of finely cut dark green leaves with branching heads of purple thistle-like flowers.

The erodiums were described earlier under mid-season plants but I find that they generally have a long flowering period and frequently are among the most colourful plants on the rock garden towards the end of the season. This especially applies to some of the larger species suggested for growing among shrubs and larger perennials.

3 Alpines for Shade

Early Season

Many gardeners seem to look on shade as a 'problem area' and I hope that the number of plants described in this chapter will reassure them. It has always seemed to me that shade-loving plants have a special delicacy and charm which is lacking in the generally more garish sun-lovers, and I think that if I were given the choice of an all-shady or an all-sunny garden I would probably opt for the former. Many of the plants are natural woodlanders, but others are natives of high rainfall areas where the atmosphere is always damp, and both groups resent the few long hot spells which we occasionally enjoy living in the south of England. Shade is essential for them here, but it becomes gradually less necessary further north, until in Scotland you find that many of the plants described can be grown in full sun.

Preparation of the ground is vital and I have discussed this in the first chapter. I have assumed, in recommending suitable plants, that they will be given a position which has had plenty of humus incorporated and is not full of roots, or too heavily overhung by tree branches. If you have to deal with dry shade the choice of plants is much more limited, and I shall try to mention those likely to tolerate it.

Although the plants are grouped as in the previous chapter, there are many more shrubs that enjoy shade, and to a considerable extent these will take the place of the plentiful easy-carpeters of open situations.

Easy Carpeters

In the earliest months of the year it is again the bulbs which will provide much of the impact in the garden, especially those which are vigorous enough to build up into drifts of colour, to convince the gardener that spring is on the way. The flowering year for me starts with winter aconites, *Eranthis hyemalis*, which quickly increase and seed themselves around in any shady spot, to give a sea of yellow beneath the shrubs which will flower later. They are really a little too vigorous for the rock garden, or anywhere they compete with smaller alpines, and I prefer to plant them with groups of daffodils and other easy bulbs, such as scillas and chionodoxas, which will carry on the flowering season into April.

At the same time the more vigorous snowdrops, *Galanthus nivalis*, *G. caucasicus* and *G. elwesii*, will provide patches of white among the blues and yellows, and there are also some less common species which are suitable for rock gardens. I find the snowdrops have quite a long season, and before they are over the first anemones are appearing, even in quite dense shade. Among my favourites are the pale blue or white *Anemone apennina*, and many forms of our native wood anemone, *A. nemorosa*, which vary in colour from white to deep lavender. The low-growing *Anemone ranunculoides* makes a carpet of small deep yellow flowers in the same conditions, so that you can enjoy beautiful drifts of white, yellow or blue anemones to brighten up the darker corners of the garden after the aconites and early snowdrops are over. The varieties of *Anemone blanda*, blue, pink or white, are equally effective but do better in partial shade or in full sun. I find they spread more slowly than the shade-loving species, but they grow particularly well in chalky soils.

Chionodoxas and scillas are generally considered to be sun-lovers, but they seem to thrive in partial shade. In my own garden, after some seventeen years, they have indeed become a mild menace, seeding themselves throughout a shrub border, which becomes a sea of blue in March and April, but less welcome when the ground is covered with their decaying leaves and seed pods!

Although I am not including them as alpines, and certainly not as carpeters, the hellebores play a vital role in these shady borders, enjoying the same conditions and flowering at the same time as many of the bulbs mentioned. Their flowers are so long-lasting that they can usually be enjoyed throughout the major part of the bulb season, and still look attractive when the larger shrubs are coming into bloom.

CARDAMINE AND DENTARIA

I group these together, as the genus *Dentaria* has largely been sunk into *Cardamine* (but may well remain under its better-known name in nursery catalogues). In general, they grow between 6–12 in (15–30 cm) and spread gently undergound – less gently if you provide them with ideal humus-rich conditions. The flowers, typical of Cruciferae, are like those of our Lady's Smock, but in colours varying from white, through creamy-yellow, to purple in the species generally available. At the height of a summer border's season they might be considered weedy, but as early-flowering easy plants for dark shady places among shrubs, they are very useful; in fact, I am always surprised how often visitors to my garden enquire about them.

Cardamine trifolia is different from the others in having neat evergreen trifoliate leaves, gradually building up into a low mound, with short sprays of pure white flowers in spring. The more spreading herbaceous species include *Cardamine pentaphyllos* (*Dentaria digitata*) with purple flowers, *C. enneaphyllos* and *C. kitaibelii* (*Dentaria polyphylla*) with creamy-yellow flowers, and *C. heptaphylla* (*D. pinnata*), which generally has white flowers, but these again may be purple in some forms.

The flowering period of these plants is generally April to early May, so that they follow after the wealth of early bulbs and before the main flowering of shrubs.

PULMONARIA

Pulmonarias are generally regarded as border plants rather than alpines, maybe because they are too robust for the rock garden, spreading rapidly in humus-rich soil in the shade of shrubs. They vary in height from 6–18 in (15–45 cm), and in colour, which can be blue, pink or white, the blues usually with a reddish tinge. They are invaluable for early-flowering ground cover even in difficult conditions and contrast well with some of the more vigorous narcissi. Their spreading capabilities make them unsuitable for associating with more dainty subjects.

Various colour forms will be found in catalogues, from which a choice can be made. Many have attractively pale-spotted leaves, or even silver leaves in *Pulmonaria saccharata* 'Argentea', which unfortunately has wishy-washy off-pink flowers, but which I would recommend growing for its foliage alone. *P. longifolia* is my favourite species with well-spotted leaves and excellent sprays of true blue flowers, a little later in spring than most of the others.

EPIMEDIUM AND VANCOUVERIA

Epimedium is another useful genus with attractive foliage from early spring to autumn, when the leaves die for the winter but are usually retained on the plant until the new leaves appear with the flowers in spring. It is as well to remove the old leaves before this, as they tend to conceal the flowers. There are many species, which all have dainty butterfly-like flowers on the thinnest of stems, above or among the leaves. In some species the leaves have a reddish tinge, which usually develops more strongly in autumn. A choice can be made from catalogues or from nurserymen's displays, but they will all make excellent ground cover for partial or full shade in acid or alkaline soils. *Epimedium grandiflorum* 'Nanum' is the daintiest and probably the smallest of all, suitable for a special place in the peat bed or shady part of the rock garden. The flowers are white, faintly tinged with purple, in April or early May. 'Rose Glow' and 'White Queen' are excellent larger varieties of *E. grandiflorum*, with pink and white flowers respectively. *E. pinnatum* is another large species up to 18 in (45 cm) high with semi-evergreen leaves (that is losing them in the coldest winters) and sprays of yellow flowers. *E. alpinum* is about half this size with red and yellow flowers, and its hybrid *E. × rubrum* is somewhat larger in all its parts. One of the best white-flowered epimediums is *E. × youngianum* 'Niveum', its flowers well-poised above the leaves.

The vancouverias are very similar good spreading plants for light or deep shade. The species usually available are *V. hexandra* with white flowers, and *V. chrysantha* with yellow flowers. The latter has a reputation for spreading excessively, but I find that in rather poor dry conditions among robust shrubs it is remaining within bounds.

RANUNCULUS FICARIA

The lesser celandine is one of our more ineradicable weeds, but this should not put anyone off buying some of its excellent well-behaved named varieties,

69

Figure 16   Epimedium grandiflorum 'Nanum'

which have the same small leaves on low-growing plants and typical small buttercup flowers in shades between white and yellow, single or double.

The most exciting is a recent introduction by Christopher Lloyd, well named 'Brazen Hussy', with deep chocolate-purple iridescent leaves and contrasting brilliant deep yellow flowers. The single white var. *albus*, pale yellow 'Primrose', and copper-coloured var. *cuprea*, differ only in colour and much more gradual rate of increase. There are several double yellow forms including 'Colarette', with a green centre which varies in size but always makes a nice contrast to the yellow flowers.

SAXIFRAGA

There is one group of easy shade-loving saxifrages which flower in April and May, the so-called 'mossies'. These vary in their ultimate spread, but all make a low carpet of mossy rosettes if planted in well-drained soil in at least partial shade. They are much less vigorous than the pulmonarias and are easy to keep within bounds. Indeed, the smaller ones like the golden-leaved 'Cloth of Gold' are useful on the rock garden, whereas I prefer to use the more spreading varieties as an edging to a shady border or even among shrubs. Although associating happily with rhododendrons they will grow equally well in limy soils where ericaceous plants are impossible, as long as conditions are not too dry for them.

A wide choice of different varieties is available, and a colour range from white, through shades of pink, to deep red. Most alpine nurserymen have a good selection. I am especially fond of the variety 'Bob Hawkins', which has somewhat unexciting white flowers but makes an intriguing carpet of beautifully variegated green and yellow rosettes, attractive at all seasons.

Typical Alpines

When considering the 'easy carpeters' for shade, bulbous plants were the season's openers, and I confined myself to those sufficiently robust to play their part in this way. Among the remaining shade-loving bulbs are some of the most beautiful of all alpine plants. What can compare with the beauty of the erythroniums and trilliums, which flower in March and April and revel in reasonably well-drained rich soil with plenty of humus, preferably leaf-mould, which is never allowed to dry out? Given such conditions, if planted and left alone, these species will gradually increase into substantial clumps. In those fortunate gardens with woodland conditions they will thrive among trees and shrubs, as long as the ground does not become too full of roots. In smaller gardens the peat bed is the ideal situation, or well-prepared areas between the smaller ericaceous shrubs whose roots will not encroach on them too quickly.

The erythroniums start flowering in March and continue well into April. Any species can be recommended with their exquisite flowers and recurving petals nodding on thin stems above their glossy leaves, which with their pale mottling are frequently attractive in themselves. Some of the easiest and best are *E. tuolumnense* with deep yellow flowers, 'White Beauty' and *E. oregonum* with white flowers, *E. revolutum*, a wonderful rather taller plant with pink flowers and mottled leaves, and the best-known, usually pink-flowered *E. dens-canis*. Curiously, I have always found the first four easy to grow in my peat bed, whereas *E. dens-canis* is slow to increase and also reluctant to flower.

Towards the end of the erythronium season the trilliums begin to flower and usually continue into early May. These have large three-lobed leaves and three-petalled flowers, differing considerably in shape. As in *Erythronium* they are all very worthwhile. *Trillium grandiflorum* and *T. ovatum* are among the best, with large pure white flowers, the former having a rare and exceptionally fine pale pink form. In *T. sessile* the flowers are sessile upon the leaves, forming a long upturned cup, which is usually reddish-brown but is creamy-white in some forms. The same reddish-brown colour is seen in *T. erectum* but the flowers are nodding above the leaves, with reflecting petals, and again there is a creamy-yellow form available, a better colour for dark corners. Several other species are sometimes available, especially a delightful miniature, *Trillium rivale*, only 2–3 in (5–8 cm) high, with dainty white flowers, in some forms heavily spotted with pink at the base of the petals. Although it is small and delicate-looking I find it grows well in the peat bed, and all the trilliums are happier in the garden than in pots.

Cyclamen coum is one of the easiest spring-flowering bulbs to establish in the shade of trees and shrubs and it will tolerate dry and less rich conditions than the other bulbs mentioned. It is easy to establish if growing corms with roots attached are planted. The dried corms often offered in the autumn are poor value, as they may have been lifted from the wild and are reluctant to start into growth. Once established they will seed themselves around, or the seed can be taken off the plant when ripe in July and sown in pots or boxes, to grow on for a couple of years before planting out. A well-established colony under shrubs or deciduous trees is a wonderful sight for any garden, with a fine range of colour and leaf forms. The leaves can be glossy green and unmarked, they can be streaked and spotted with white or, in the 'Pewter' group, there can be an even grey colour over most of the surface. The flower colour varies from white, usually with a pink 'nose', through shades of pink to deepest magenta. Flowering often starts in late January and can continue into April. The season can be extended by planting *Cyclamen repandum* with its deep rose flowers, but this species may prove a little tender and is certainly less easy to establish.

I have a long narrow bed partially shaded by a box hedge, which was planted some fifteen years ago with nothing but cyclamen: *C. coum*, *C. hederifolium*, *C. purpurascens* and *C. repandum*. Now it is one of the greatest joys in the garden, with a carpet of *C. coum* in the spring and a carpet of *C. hederifolium* in the autumn, and beautifully marbled leaves throughout the winter and spring. *C. purpurascens* gradually disappeared, but there remains a patch of *C. repandum* tucked well under the lea of the hedge to give a sprinkling of late flowers when the *C. coum* are over.

Some corydalis were mentioned as early sun-lovers, but several species do better in good shady conditions, especially if the soil is well-drained as well as rich. Perhaps the finest of all is *Corydalis cashmeriana*, a small plant with flowers of a wonderful brilliant blue. Like so many Himalayan plants, this is undoubtedly easier in Scotland and the midland and northern counties, but it can be grown in the south in a gritty peat bed which is never allowed to dry out. *Corydalis ambigua* is larger, up to 6 in (15 cm) high, and in its best form has flowers of similar, but paler, blue. I find this much easier to grow than *C. cashmeriana* and it has formed a good colony here, growing among trilliums and erythroniums. Unlike *C. cashmeriana*, it sets seed and so is much easier to propagate. The uncommon *Corydalis bracteata* enjoys similar conditions and has deep yellow flowers with large toothed bracts.

So far, all the plants I have described have been bulbous or rhizomatous, because these play such an important part in providing early colour in the shady garden. Whereas most of the early-flowering non-bulbous sun-lovers belong to a few large genera, most of the other shade-lovers, apart from shrubs, belong to small genera, each with a few species, so that it is more difficult to describe them under broad headings.

At a time when we are still enjoying the early bulbs, *Hacquetia epipactis* also begins its long flowering period. It unfurls its aconite-like leaves soon after Christmas, and before these leaves are fully developed the flowers open on 1–2 in (2–5 cm) stems. Although they have the appearance of green flowers with a broad central boss of yellow, it is the tiny flowers themselves which form the

Figure 17   Corydalis cashmeriana

centre, surrounded by a ring of large green bracts. The 'flowers' last in good conditions for weeks on end, until the leaves eventually lengthen and hide them. Although not a spectacular plant, it is one I would hate to be without, easily grown in any shady spot and seeding itself quite freely, so there are always spare plants for friends.

Some time in March the much more spectacular flowers of the Canadian bloodroot, *Sanguinaria canadensis*, appear. It forms a mat of thick rhizomatous roots just beneath the surface of the soil, which exude red juice if they are cut – hence the common name. The attractive grey-green leaves appear in the spring, beginning to unfurl at the same time as the flowers open, pure white and single, very similar to a ranunculus, with conspicuous yellow stamens. This describes the single form, but in fact the double *Sanguinaria canadensis* 'Plena' is much more popular, with fully double pure white globular flowers. It is so beautiful that everyone wants to grow it, and it presents few problems in rich woodland soil. Unfortunately, it has a very short flowering season, usually little more than a week or ten days. On the other hand the leaves also are very attractive and last for a couple of months before dying down again.

Japan has been a source of several exquisite shade-loving plants, none more beautiful than *Jeffersonia dubia*, which makes a cluster of purple-tinged lobed leaves on long slender stems, with fine lavender-blue flowers on 6 in (15 cm) stems among the leaves. It is slow-growing, but will gradually make a sizeable

Figure 18   Jeffersonia dubia

clump in good conditions. *Jeffersonia diphylla* is sometimes offered – a white-flowered species which does not quite attain the beauty of *J. dubia*.

Somewhat later-flowering, sometimes into our mid-season, is another wonderful Japanese woodlander, *Glaucidium palmatum*, a herbaceous plant with large acer-like leaves, gradually developing during spring and early summer, and very large poppy-like lavender flowers. A beautiful white variety is occasionally seen. The leaves of the podophyllums are similar to those of the glaucidium, except that they have beautiful reddish markings. The podophyllum's white or pale pink flowers are smaller but they are followed by very large dangling red fruits. Both the glaucidium and the podophyllums become a little large for the rock garden once they are well-established in suitable soil. The leaves will eventually attain up to 2 ft (60 cm) and are large enough to swamp smaller plants. I like to grow them in groups among larger shrubs or among meconopsis and candelabra primulas, which will flower a week or two later.

Unfortunately, the most beautiful of all Japanese woodlanders, the shortias, are difficult to establish, at least in the drier southern counties. However, they can be grown even in Kent, and I now have several reasonably contented clumps in full shade in a peat bed, which is watered when necessary during dry spells. There are three species and some varieties. They all form low clumps of leathery glossy leaves, tinted with red to a greater or lesser degree especially in the autumn, and have clusters of white to deep pink flowers on short stems.

Shortia uniflora has large pink frilled flowers. In *S. galacifolia*, the only North American species, the white flowers are smaller and more funnel-shaped. The most exciting of all is *S. soldanelloides* and its varieties, with deep reddish bell-shaped flowers, the petals beautifully fringed like those of the soldanellas.

The soldanellas themselves must surely be the most admired of all true alpines by anyone who has seen them in the European Alps, pushing their noses through the melting snow in early spring. Unfortunately, they are not the easiest plants to grow well, partly because they seem to be the favourite food of every slug in the garden, and partly because the buds tend to abort – or are they eaten – before the stems can lengthen in the spring. All the species have similar flowers, nodding bells with frilled tips on dainty stalks only one inch (2.5 cm) high in the tiny *Soldanella minima*, and up to 4 in (10 cm) in the larger species *S. alpina*, *S. montana* and *S. villosa*. In my experience, the easiest of these is *S. villosa*, which grows satisfactorily in a gritty pocket of my peat bed and always seems to produce a few of its deep lavender flowers. There is one other species intermediate in size, *S. carpatica*, which I find flowers more freely, though it is slow growing. Best of all is its exquisite white form, *S. carpatica* var. *alba*.

Hepaticas have been grown by enthusiasts for many years, and there were probably considerably more varieties available fifty years ago than there are now. They used to be included in the genus *Anemone*, and their flowers are very similar, but the clusters of three-lobed leaves are quite distinct. The flowers, on 2–6 in (5–15 cm) stems, are usually deep lavender in colour and single, but double lavender, single and double pink and single and double white are sometimes available. For some reason they never flourish in my garden and

Figure 19   Shortia soldanelloides

75

I cast envious eyes at the substantial clumps with hundreds of flowers which I see in other gardens. I am sure they do best in a heavy loam, which can be limy, and they never seem to flourish on light sandy soils.

Ramondas and haberleas are almost unique in their preference for a shady wall. They have large rosettes in which water can collect unless they are planted on their sides, so that a north-facing retaining wall, or a wall shaded by trees, suits them to perfection. Given such a position they are easy to grow and long-lasting. I have a low wall retaining a peat bed and its entire length has been planted with groups of these two genera, which have increased and flowered regularly for the last sixteen years without any attention.

The ramondas form large rosettes of flat crinkly leaves from which the flowering stems appear in late April and May. The stems are usually about 4 in (10 cm) long, with several beautiful flat-faced flowers with overlapping petals, pale lavender in the commonest species, *Ramonda myconi*, but pink or white in its varieties. Two other species, *R. serbica* and *R. nathaliae*, are very similar, with lavender flowers.

The haberleas also form large rosettes, increasing much more freely than the ramondas, the leaves larger and narrower with toothed edges. The flowers are tubular, opening widely at their mouths, their basic colour a soft lavender blue with yellow markings on the lip in *Haberlea rhodopensis* and in the larger-flowered *H. ferdinandi-coburgi*. There is also an excellent albino in *H. rhodopensis* 'Virginale', with white flowers similarly marked with yellow.

Many of the vast range of primulas do better in shady conditions with good drainage and plenty of humus. The most important group – the Candelabra section – will be described later (see p. 104) as they reach their peak in June, but most of the Farinosa section flower as early as April. These are small plants, not very long-lived, but easily raised from seed, which can be grown in small numbers in the peat bed, in shady pockets in the rock garden, or can be planted in larger numbers among shrubs or in the front of a shady border.

The most widely grown is our native bird's-eye primrose, *P. farinosa*, with rosettes of heavily farinose leaves and 3–4 in (7–10 cm) stems bearing clusters of pale pink, yellow-eyed flowers. *P. frondosa* is similar on a larger scale, and there are one or two other species, for instance *P. modesta* and *P. modesta* var. *fauriae*, which are tiny inch-high miniatures. These can all be relied on to set seed, so that they are easily replaced as they die out. Two or three years seems to be their usual life-span in my garden.

One of the most fascinating groups of primulas is the Petiolaris section, a source of despair in southern counties but much more amenable if you garden in a part of the country with high rainfall and high humidity in summer. They are all such exquisitely beautiful early-flowering plants that they tempt every-one to grow them, even in hot dry counties like Kent! Summer rather than winter creates the problems and if, like me, you want to 'kick against the pricks' rather than forget them, I suggest that the best chance is to grow them in full shade in very rich soil with abundant drainage and spray them with water as frequently as possible during warm spells. They also seem to exhaust their soil

Figure 20   Primula whitei

quickly and are best divided frequently and replanted in a freshly-prepared bed with plenty of leaf mould, compost, or well-rotted manure incorporated.

There are many Petiolaris species available for the enthusiast. Perhaps the most beautiful and easiest is *P. whitei* with ice-blue flowers with a conspicuous white eye. *P. sonchifolia* is somewhat similar in colour but harder to please. *P. gracilipes* is another comparatively easy species, which differs in having deep rose flowers, and *P. aureata* has deep yellow flowers with a white eye.

In Scotland and the northern English counties these primulas have much greater possibilities, growing 'like cabbages' in good conditions, so that they can be grouped among shrubs or among taller perennials such as meconopsis, lilies and nomocharis, which thrive in just the same conditions and flower after the primulas are over.

Primula sieboldii from Japan is another woodland species which enjoys just the same conditions, but even in Kent it has proved quite easy to grow if its basic requirements are satisfied. I have found it almost too easy for the properly prepared peat bed, as it has gradually spread to a patch a couple of feet square. Another patch is thriving in the shade of a wall with the simple incorporation of abundant peat and some compost.

Varieties of *Primula sieboldii* have been bred for years in Japan and there is a good choice available from nurseries. The plants die down in winter, generally coming into growth in March with pale green hairy lobed leaves. They usually start flowering towards the end of our period, with umbels of six to twelve flowers on stems usually about 6–8 in (15–20 cm) high, but varying with conditions and the different clones. The commonest colours are pale pink or white, but the full range includes deep rose and pale to deep lilac blue. It is a mystery to me why these beautiful, easy plants are not more widely grown.

A few other primulas may start their season as early as this, but their main flowering period is in May or June and they will be described in the mid-season section (see p. 106), together with their close allies the dodecatheons.

Shrubs

Most of the early season shrubs flower in April, May and the beginning of June. They have a very important part to play in shady areas, especially for gardeners on acid soils. Unfortunately, it is one area in which gardeners on chalk can justifiably feel deprived, because nearly all of these shrubs are lime-hating members of the Ericaceae. If you garden on chalk I am convinced that it is not worth struggling with these plants, except in containers; you will have to make more use of polygalas, daphnes and the non-shrubby plants described elsewhere.

The ericaceous shrubs available are a huge group, which includes the rhododendrons, and they all have similar requirements in general: an acid soil with abundant humus, especially leaf mould, semi-shady conditions at least in the hotter counties, and plenty of moisture at all times – the mixture as before, in fact! They can be any height from one inch (2.5 cm) to large trees, and their use in the garden depends mainly on their size.

The smallest shrubs look lost in the shade of large rhododendrons and I prefer to plant them in a peat bed or a special shady pocket in the rock garden, where they can be admired at close range among other small plants of similar requirements: for example, the smaller erythroniums, trilliums, corydalis, primulas, etc. The larger dwarf shrubs, 8 in (20 cm) or more high, look more in keeping between their taller relations or any of the more statuesque perennials such as meconopsis and lilies, as an alternative to the robust carpeting plants previously described.

Among the most exciting of the small ericaceous plants are the cassiopes and phyllodoces, which look interesting at all times of the year and have a very special delicate charm when they are in flower in late spring and early summer. Cassiopes all have thin whipcord stems, some thicker and more upright than others, and small bell-shaped white flowers. They are not altogether easy to please, because in Southern counties they grow well in full shade but tend to flower sparsely, whereas if you plant them in drier sunny positions, their shoots frequently turn brown at the base and you are faced with a much less attractive but more free-flowering plant. In cooler areas I think it is better to grow them in full sun as long as the ground is kept moist. Here in Kent they have been reasonably successful at the edge of a peat bed which becomes sunny at midsummer, because it is shaded by a wall which is not quite high enough! I thought this might be disastrous, but the peat bed is very near a water supply so

I can keep it extra moist around midsummer, and the added light seems to benefit the cassiopes without scorching them.

There are several *Cassiope* species and an increasing number of hybrids available, but many of them are very similar to each other and I suspect only the specialist would want to grow them all. *Cassiope lycopodioides* and *C. mertensiana* are excellent easy species of very slender growth, with the latter rather less compact. *Cassiope selaginoides* and *C. tetragona* are more upright with thicker stems, and are not generally so easy to please. *C. wardii* is also upright with thick, very hairy stems, and is very difficult to grow and propagate. I think that some of the vigorous hybrids are the best choices for the garden, combining healthy growth with abundant flowering. Among those which I have found satisfactory here are 'Edinburgh', 'Muirhead', 'Randle Cook' and 'Badenoch'. None of these beautiful shrubs will get too large, and they are ideal for the peat garden.

The phyllodoces seem to me to be more satisfactory garden plants, as they always flower well and have healthy foliage as long as they are given the well-prepared position suggested. The colour range is greater – pink to red, white, or yellow. Probably the commonest and most satisfactory is *Phyllodoce coerulea*, which builds up into a spreading bush only 6–8 in (15–20 cm) high, with heather-like leaves and abundant deep rosy-purple bell-shaped flowers in late spring. My favourite is the dainty Japanese *P. nipponica*, a very small upright-growing bush with pure white bells with contrasting reddish calyces. It is supposedly more difficult, but seems reasonably easy here in the peat bed in almost complete shade. *P. breweri* and *P.* × *intermedia* have flowers of a similar colour to *P. coerulea*, but are taller-growing rather coarser plants. There are also two beautiful yellow-flowered species, *P. aleutica* and *P. glanduliflora*, which are similar in size to *P. coerulea* but a little slower-growing.

The genus *Phyllodoce* has given rise to several bigeneric hybrids. The best known until recently was *Phyllothamnus erectus*, a hybrid with the very rare and difficult *Rhodothamus chamaecistus*. This is an upright-growing shrub, not usually more than 12 in (30 cm) high, with clusters of deep rose flowers at the tips of the stems. Recently hybrids with *Kalmiopsis leachiana* have become available, the commonest *Phylliopsis* × *hillieri* 'Pinocchio', and more recently 'Coppelia'. These are excellent shrubs, closely resembling the phyllodoces, and they flower so freely that they make a real splash of deep reddish-pink in late April and May.

Kalmiopsis leachiana itself is a comparatively recent introduction from the north-west USA, which is usually seen as a carefully nurtured alpine-house plant, but I have been growing it successfully for several years in the peat bed. It is a very beautiful dwarf evergeen with abundant saucer-shaped pale pink flowers in April, and will take several years to grow more than 8 in (20 cm) high.

One of the most diminutive of all these ericaceous shrubs is *Arcterica nana*, a beautiful little plant which gradually makes a spreading carpet, only 2 in (5 cm) high, of glossy box-like leaves, above which rise short spikes of white bell-shaped flowers. Although it roots as it goes, it is never invasive, only spreading an inch or two a year.

Another plant of somewhat similar habit but on a much larger scale is *Vaccinium nummularia*, one of my favourite ericaceae but slightly tender. It grows to about 12 in (30 cm) high and spreads quickly by suckers in really good conditions, so much so that I have been quite pleased to have it curbed by hard winters every few years. The stems are intensely hairy with very glossy small leaves, and the abundant flowers, typically bell-shaped, are pale pink deepening at their tips. Another good vaccinium, but maybe a little large, is *V. glauco-album*, which is worth growing for its foliage alone. The leaves are large, rounded, and deep green, but the new young growth is a pale bluish-green which quickly becomes flushed with pink, retaining this colour for several weeks. It has a reputation for tenderness, but I have found it as least as hardy as *V. nummularia* here in Kent.

Vaccinium vitis-idaea is another excellent low-growing species, especially in its variety 'Minor'. A word of warning! In good peat-bed conditions the type species especially can be a menace, and I find it suckering disastrously far through other small plants. It is very attractive, with tiny leaves and spikes of pink-flushed flowers, but I suggest growing it in more ordinary acid soil among other shrubs, or stick to the 'Minor' form if you want it in your best peat bed.

Leiophyllum buxifolium is somewhat similar, but it is taller and, in my experience, it does not sucker, so it is perfectly safe to grow it among smaller plants. My own plant after some five years has made an upright bush about 10 in (25 cm) high and of similar width, with small evergreen leaves along its woody stems, and fine heads of tiny pink-flushed flowers in May. It is always one of the most floriferous of the group, making a striking splash of colour when it flowers with the trilliums and earliest rhododendrons.

Ledum is a small genus of ericaceous shrubs which can be used in the same way as the leiophyllums. They have larger leaves and somewhat looser growth, but again they produce conspicuous heads of white flowers in spring. The most common species is *Ledum groenlandicum*, which may become a little large after several years, and should be placed among taller plants. However, it has a much neater form 'Compactum', which I would not hesitate to plant in the peat garden.

The genus *Andromeda* is one of the most beautiful of all the Ericaceae. The species generally available is *A. polyfolia*, but it has many varieties, which vary in height up to 2 ft (60 cm). In choosing these look out for the most compact, which make neat bushes of small grey-green leaves with recurved margins and have clusters of pink or occasionally white bells, which are especially large for the size of the plant in the best forms. Names to look out for are 'Compacta' and 'Compacta alba', 'Nana', 'Minima' and some recently introduced Japanese hybrids with clonal names such as 'Nikko' and 'Shibutsu'.

You will have noticed that all the shrubs mentioned are evergreen and have small white or pink bell-shaped flowers. In addition, many of them have fine

Figure 21   Andromeda polyfolia

fruits, which are at their best in the autumn. I propose to describe those, notably the gaultherias and pernettyas, in a later section (see p. 113), although they also have white flowers earlier in the year.

RHODODENDRONS

Here we have a genus which has revolutionised gardening on acid soil during the last hundred years, becoming the backbone, if not the whole essence, of many famous gardens. Although the larger species and hybrids have taken pride of place in this revolution, there are a vast number of dwarf species, sufficient indeed to be the subject of books of considerable size. With this extraordinary range of plants available it is difficult to make a choice, and the ideal method is probably to visit some of the gardens with a good collection open to the public, notably the Savill and Valley Gardens at Windsor and the RHS Gardens at Wisley in the south, and Ness Gardens and the Royal Botanic Gardens, Edinburgh, in the north. At these gardens it will be possible to assess not only their beauty of flower and foliage, but their ultimate size in the garden. Here I shall describe a few of my own favourite dwarfs, a very limited choice from a garden in which rhododendrons only play a minor part. This is not to decry their usefulness, because, in addition to a marvellous period of glory in April and May, their interesting evergreen foliage can be valuable at all seasons, especially if this feature is particularly considered when choosing them.

My personal view is that rhododendrons en masse can be boring, particularly the smaller species grown together with little height-variation, and it is much more exciting to grow them in small groups or as individuals, widely spaced with other plants between them. These can include the taller shrubs needing similar conditions, such as *Enkianthus*, eucryphias, stewartias or magnolias, or the smaller woodland bulbs such as trilliums and erythroniums, as well as 'carpeting plants' and other shade-loving plants such as primulas, meconopsis and many lilies. Bear in mind that many of the dwarf rhododendrons flower better and keep their compact growth better in full sun, but they require moisture at all times so a compromise may be necessary – grow them in partial shade in drier conditions and in full sun in the north or west.

Although there is a very comprehensive and complicated classification of rhododendrons, it seems simpler here, when considering a small selection and their use in the garden, to group them according to colour.

I have always had a weakness for yellow rhododendrons, large or small, and I am surprised that they are not more widely-grown in small gardens. Most of them enjoy partial shade, so that they will brighten dark corners with their pale flowers, their own dark leaves making an excellent background. One of the best really small species is *Rhododendron keiskii*, a variable plant with one superb clone 'Yaku Fairy', which makes a spreading bush not more than 6–8 in (15–20 cm) high, smothered in large yellow flowers in April. *R. hanceanum* is another excellent dwarf species with smaller flowers and less spreading growth. Another favourite yellow-flowered species is *R. sargentianum*, which is a very compact-growing small-leaved shrub with heads of small yellow flowers. It is one of the most beautiful of this group and, in spite of a reputation for being more difficult to grow, it has proved quite satisfactory here in Kent, growing in partial shade among larger shrubs.

In addition to these species, several beautiful dwarf hybrids have been raised, two of the best being 'Chikor' and 'Curlew'. All these yellow-flowered rhododendrons look particularly good planted in groups with the blue-flowered species, of which there is a wide choice.

The blue rhododendrons also vary greatly in height, but most of them will eventually become taller than the smallest yellows. *R. impeditum* is one of the easiest and most compact, with tiny leaves and clusters of small deep blue flowers. This takes several years to attain 12 in (30 cm), whereas most of the other species will eventually attain a metre or more – for example, *R. fastigiatum*, *R. hippophaeoides* and *R. russatum*, and the excellent hybrids 'Blue Diamond' and 'Blue Tit'.

The choice of white-flowered dwarfs is more limited. One of the earliest flowering species of all is *R. leucaspis*, which is usually grown in the alpine house as it is susceptible to frost, but it can be grown in the open in sheltered gardens. It has large, widely open white flowers with conspicuous brown anthers, and but for its bud tenderness would be one of the most popular species. The taller growing *R. microleucum* has tiny leaves and trusses of several small white flowers, which are much more frost-resistant. It is slow-growing, up to a couple of feet. 'Ptarmigan' is an excellent early-flowering white hybrid between *R. microleucum* and *R. leucaspis*, which makes a low spreading bush. One of the most successful white-flowered species growing in my peat bed is the late-flowering *R. kiusianum* 'Album', another low spreading shrub which is allied to the azaleas. It is semi-deciduous with comparatively large white flowers in May.

Most of the remaining species to be described here have flowers in shades of pink, red and purple. Pale pink is one of the most beautiful colours for the spring garden, combining well with the blue of the later-flowering bulbs such as *Anemone apennina* and the scillas and chionodoxas. Unfortunately, the earliest-flowering rhododendrons are much more susceptible to frost than are the bulbs. One of the earliest worth planting in sheltered gardens is *Rhododendron* × *cilpinense* with large pale pink flowers that are very susceptible to frost, although the bush itself withstands the cold well. It can attain 2–3 ft (60–90 cm) quite quickly and so is not a true dwarf, but I enjoy it as a contrast to the early bulbs, when we are lucky enough to have a few frost-free days at the crucial moment – perhaps one year in two here! I think this is well worth trying, but if the gamble is not for you, a similar colour is seen in the much hardier April-flowering *R. pemakoense*, a marvellous true dwarf, which hides its small leaves beneath a mass of large pink flowers. It flowers in my garden in a peat bed at the same time as the erythroniums, a striking contrast to the pale cream of *Erythronium oregonum*, and surprisingly pleasing next to the deep yellow of *E. tuolumnense*. Yellow and pink can be horrid, especially with daffodils under a pink magnolia, but I think the orange cups are the problem there! *R. racemosum* is an even tougher (but to my taste less beautiful) species, with rather sparse upright growth and heads of several small pale pink flowers with prominent anthers. It is a very variable plant, so look out for the most compact forms – I suspect mine is not one of them.

Various forms of *Rhododendron campylogynum* are available, and they are all excellent compact shrubs, dwarf enough to grow in the peat garden with smaller shade-loving alpines. All these dwarf rhododendrons are very easy to move, with their dense fibrous rootball, so that once they become too large for their neighbours they can be moved elsewhere, preferably in early spring or autumn. The colour of *R. campylogynum* is very variable, including a delicate pale pink, creamy white, deep magenta and most shades in between. They are all neat and floriferous, with flowers of an attractive bell shape. *R. cephalanthum*, especially in its beautiful var. *crebreflorum*, is similar in habit with particularly beautiful pale pink flowers.

Rhododendron trichostomum belongs to an interesting group, of which *R. sargentianum* is another, which has unusual flower trusses resembling those of the daphne – clusters of small tubular flowers in a tight head. It is a variable species usually taller and more upright-growing than *R. campylogynum*, with white or pale pink flowers.

Some of the most spectacular large rhododendrons are the brilliant red species and hybrids. This colour is also found in a few dwarfs which have been hybridised to produce such 'semi-dwarfs' as the famous 'Elizabeth'. This is often planted as a dwarf, but care must be taken if it is planted among small alpines as it will quickly overshadow them and must be moved before any damage is done. On the other hand, its parent *R. forrestii* is a ground-hugging shrub only attaining 6–8 in (15–20 cm) at the most. It is not at all free-flowering and its variety *repens* should be grown, similar in habit but more generous in producing its large blood-red bells. 'Carmen' is a more compact hybrid than 'Elizabeth', with flowers of an amazingly deep red, so dark that it does not show up well against a dark background.

One of the most beautiful and most dwarf of all is the deciduous *R. camschaticum*. This runs gently underground and has large pale green leaves and large short-stemmed purplish-red flowers in April. Although it has a reputation for being tricky it seems here to enjoy peat-bed conditions, and spreads gently by layering itself around. I mentioned earlier *R. kiusianum* var. 'Album' as a late-flowering dwarf, which belongs to the azalea series. *R. nakaharai* is a fairly recent introduction with which I am very impressed. It is one of the smallest and certainly the latest-flowering of all the 'azaleas'. It forms a spreading bush 4–6 in (10–15 cm) high, with masses of comparatively large brick-red flowers in July or even later, giving some bright colour to the peat bed when most of the other flowering plants are over, apart from the Asiatic gentians.

To complete this limited selection I would recommend *R. radicans*, a tiny prostrate shrub, which will spread sideways gradually but is never more than an inch or two above the ground, even when it produces its clusters of deep purple flowers in April or May.

LIME-TOLERANT SHRUBS

There are surprisingly few early-flowering shrubs, other than the Ericaceae, suitable for sun or for shade. Some of the daphnes described among the sun-lovers will tolerate partial shade, and those few which seem to need shade will be described in the next section, as they are unlikely to flower before May.

Some of the polygalas certainly come into this group and are excellent low-growing spreading plants of modest height. *Polygala chamaebuxus* is the most widely grown, with small glossy leaves and clusters of yellow and white flowers in spring. It seems quite easy in any semi-shady spot or in full sun in cooler areas, but its subspecies *grandiflora* is even better, with deep rose flowers with a yellow lip. This is sometimes offered in catalogues as *Polygala rhodoptera*, or *P. purpurea*, and it seems to me that the former name applies to a particularly good form of it with extra large flowers. Another species worth looking out for is *P. vayredae*. This is a smaller-leaved more compact plant, with flowers of the deepest magenta.

Mid-season (May–July)

Easy Carpeters

Among the early-flowering shade-loving alpines, I included some of the more robust bulbs with the 'easy carpeters' and mentioned that many of the shrubs

14. *Glaucidium palmatum* and *Phylliopsis hillieri* 'Pinocchio' (shade-loving/early season)

15. *Corydalis ambigua* (shade-loving/early season)

16. *Dicentra eximia* and 'Luxuriant' (shade-loving/mid-season)

17. *Phlox adsurgens* (shade-loving/early season)

18. *Rhododendron camschaticum* (shade-loving/early season)

19. *Primula vialii* (shade-loving/mid-season)

20. *Erythronium oregonum*, *Sanguinaria canadensis 'Plena'* and *Camellia* (shade-loving/early season)

could be used in the same way, as plants for the front of borders or to fill in among large shrubs and perennials.

In mid-season the vigorous spreading bulbs are over, but many of the shrubs already mentioned have still to flower, and, in addition, there is a greater choice of easy carpeting perennials, which I shall describe in alphabetical order.

ASTILBE

The larger astilbes are among the most beautiful herbaceous perennials for moist conditions, with their attractive ferny leaves, often tinged with bronze, and fine plumes of flowers in shades of white, pink, to deepest magenta. I find them irresistible, even though my only water is in a lined pond, but growing them has meant good soil preparation with lots of manure and peat, and frequent watering on the occasions when we get a hot dry summer.

Most of these astilbes are too tall to be considered here, but there are a few dwarf species which enjoy just the same conditions; in fact, it seems to me that they will flourish in rather drier parts of the garden than their larger relations. I like to use them along the edge of shady beds, mainly devoted to rhododendrons and magnolias, followed later by meconopsis and lilies. They resemble closely the larger astilbes but on a much smaller scale, growing to less than 10 in (25 cm) high with short spikes of fluffy flowers, generally deep rose in colour. *Astilbe chinensis* is typical but a little tall, and I prefer its form 'Pumila', which is an excellent dwarf. Even smaller is a plant sold under the dubious name of *Astilbe glaberrima* 'Saxatilis', with lovely bronze-tinted leaves and spires of pink flowers. In addition to these there are some beautiful named dwarf clones of *Astilbe crispa*, such as 'Perkeo', and also of *A. simplicifolia*, the latter generally somewhat larger.

Although not strictly carpeters, all these plants gradually spread sideways to cover a reasonable area and they are easily divided in the spring if you want to build up larger groups.

CORNUS CANADENSIS

I have always found this genuine carpeting plant, only a few inches high, somewhat frustrating. In many gardens it becomes almost a menace, rapidly covering large areas and putting on a fine display of its comparatively large white 'flowers'. As in the larger species of *Cornus* the flowers are in fact insignificant, but they are surrounded by four large pure white bracts. In my own garden *C. canadensis* sulks everywhere, except in a recently prepared peat bed devoted to small treasures, where it says 'thank you very much' and spreads undergound in all directions. The other frustration is that in the wild it produces a fine crop of conspicuous red berries in autumn, but here they are produced very sparsely, even in gardens where it flourishes exceedingly. *Cornus × unalaschensis* has recently appeared on the garden scene and promises to behave very similarly, but is a little larger in all its parts. It has

Figure 22   Dicentra cucullaria

already 'taken off' here and is putting up leaves at an alarming distance from its
original planting position.

DICENTRA

Here we have one of the very best genera for the shady garden, but many of its
species fall into that grey area between alpines and border plants. As they are
being considered as easy carpeters, and as they are among my favourite plants,
I will only exclude the larger *Dicentra spectabilis* and its exquisite white form,
and the interesting climber *D. scandens* and its allies, with some reservations
about the size of *D. macrantha*.

One or two species are anything but 'easy' carpeters, but can come in here for
the sake of completeness. *Dicentra pelegrina* is one of the most exquisite of all
flowering plants, a cluster of finely cut silvery-blue leaves only an inch or two
high, with solitary pale pink lyre-shaped flowers in spring, but oh so difficult
even in the alpine house! Maybe it is a little easier in the north.

The smallest of the reasonably growable species is *D. cucullaria* which is a
lovely woodland plant for the choicest position in the shady rock garden or peat
bed. It produces – fleetingly – a cluster of dainty, fernlike glaucous leaves and
spikes of dangling white typically lyre-shaped flowers. It is a most beautiful

plant, but bear in mind that it is not above ground for long so that it is only too easy to put something else on top of it during a flurry of midsummer planting! *D. canadensis* is a very similar species but a little taller.

Dicentra macrantha is another (to me!) source of frustration. It has tall stems with beautiful leaves, pale green bordered with gold, beneath which hang long drooping yellow flowers, but it is temperamental and potentially a runner. In ordinary soil in a shady place I found that it produces just one or two modest stems and, after a couple of years, is dwindling rather than increasing, whereas in the ideal conditions of the peat bed it puts up robust stems at considerable intervals, usually in the middle of something else! I am sure it needs a rich moist soil and plenty of room.

Apart from the tall *D. spectabilis* var. *alba*, the most beautiful white-flowered species are *D. formosa* 'Alba', the slightly smaller and daintier *D. eximia* 'Alba', and 'Snowflake' with similar glaucous leaves and clusters of typical pearl white 'lockets'. 'Langtrees' and 'Pearl Drops' have creamy white flowers and are much more widely spreading than these. They are most useful carpeters even in quite dry situations, as are some of the pink-flowered species such as *D. formosa* and *D. eximia* themselves, the former being the larger and more vigorous with pinkish-purple flowers. One of my favourites in this group is 'Stuart Boothman'. For many years I enjoyed a spreading clump of its exceptionally finely-cut bluish leaves and spikes of several deep rose flowers. For some reason, having been sterile for many years, it now sets seed and is becoming overgrown with more typical *D. formosa* seedlings with their coarser leaves – pleasant enough in their place but not in the same class as 'Stuart Boothman'. A recent acquisition of similar spreading habit is 'Bacchanal', which has unusually pale green leaves and the darkest reddish-purple flowers of them all – a superb introduction.

In addition to these truly carpeting plants there are several excellent recently introduced hybrids, which are easy to grow but more clump-forming and a little tall for our purpose. Among the best are the very dark-flowered 'Adrian Bloom', and the vigorous 'Luxuriant' and 'Bountiful'. All these larger dicen-tras can be grown in the herbaceous border, preferably in partial shade, but I prefer to plant them among rhododendrons and taller deciduous shrubs. Here the more spreading varieties will soon grow to cover a sizeable area, but I suggest planting the clump-formers in groups of three or more, appropriate to the space available.

DISPORUM

This small genus is closely allied to *Polygonatum*, the 'Solomon's seal', but it is not so widely grown in gardens, in spite of possessing the same modest charm on a much smaller scale.

The commonest species is *Disporum hookeri* with its form *oregonum*, which has taken over a corner of my peat bed. It runs gently underground and also seeds itself widely into this bed and into the neighbouring gravel path, always a fruitful source of seedlings of all sorts. It makes a carpet of three-lobed glossy leaves on stems up to 10 in (25 cm) high. The cream-coloured tubular bell flowers hang beneath the leaves and are followed in mid-summer by bright orange berries. *Disporum smithii* is very similar, and *D. lanuginosa* is a little taller, but the only other species seen with any frequency is *D. sessile* in its variegated form. This makes upright 1 ft (30 cm) stems of sessile leaves beautifully variegated in pale green and white. Sadly I find it tends to run about with a shoot here and there, rather than make a good clump, which would be very effective in a dark corner. So far I have not seen flowers or fruits on it!

GERANIUM

The hardy geraniums are invaluable as reliable ground-covering plants for shade, even in dry conditions, but most of the suitable species and varieties are too robust and too tall to be included here. Many of the neater plants described in Chapter 2 will also thrive in partial shade, notably *G. sanguineum* and its beautiful white form.

The tiny species from New Zealand, *G. sessilifolium*, grows well here and seeds itself around in sun or shade. It makes a clump of deep green kidney-shaped leaves and has masses of small white flowers on 2–3 in (5–8 cm) stems for several weeks during the summer. Its more popular variety 'Nigrescens' has identical flowers, with the added attraction of bronze foliage. They are not spreading plants but they do seed very freely to make an easily-controlled 'carpet'.

Our native Herb Robert, *Geranium robertianum*, is too freely seeding and small-flowered to be considered anything but a weed, but it has an attractive white form 'Album', which is worth growing among shrubs. There is also a plant in the trade under the name of *G. robertianum* 'Celtic White', which presumably is a synonym for *G. celticum* var. *album*, a perfect miniature of *G. robertianum* with attractive leaves and red stems, and plenty of small white flowers, the whole plant only 2–3 in (5–8 cm) high.

Any gardener wanting robust geraniums to cover lots of ground among large shrubs, even in poor soil conditions, should study lists of perennials for the numerous easy species that grow 1–2 ft (30–60 cm) high and can become too successful in good soil conditions. In my constant search for more space for exciting new plants, I find I am frequently digging up large areas of geranium ground-cover, which was planted ten or more years ago to cover up some of the larger gaps between newly-planted shrubs. 'Ground-cover' is undoubtedly labour-saving, but it is not necessary to use the most rapidly spreading and coarser plants to cover the ground, except perhaps in the early stages of a large garden!

HEUCHERA

Heuchera is usually looked upon as a genus of border plants, with attractive rounded leaves, sometimes with bronze tints, and 2 ft (60 cm) spikes of tiny flowers in a good range of colours between white and deepest reddish-purple.

These are excellent plants for sun or shade, but the genus also contains several species small enough for the rock garden or the front of a shady mixed border. Few of these seem to be available except as seed from the specialist societies, perhaps because their flowers are less conspicuous than those of the large hybrids. One of the best is *Heuchera micrantha*, a very variable plant that may be tiny but more often attains 18 in (45 cm) in flower, with loose sprays of abundant tiny white flowers. I have seen several of the smaller species such as *H. grossularifolia* and *H. parviflora* with short spikes of white or greenish flowers, and *H. micans* with pink flowers, growing in shady rock crevices in their native habitat, and I think perhaps the best way to grow them is in crevices of a north-facing wall with ramondas and haberleas, even though they will grow happily on the flat.

Close allies of the heucheras are the tiarellas, which are useful easy carpeters of similar habit, but with much more spreading growth. *Tiarella cordifolia* is the most widely grown, making a low mat of heart-shaped leaves, often with a bronze tinge which deepens in autumn. The spires of fluffy cream-coloured flowers appear in June and last well. *T. wherryi* is similar, but the pointed three-lobed leaves are even better marked. Both these plants are attractive as a foreground for dwarf shrubs in a shady bed.

IRIS

Most of the dwarf irises are sun-lovers, but mention was made in Chapter 2 of the most important group, which enjoys semi-shade in the south, the Californian species akin to *Iris innominata* and *I. douglasiana*. I find that in rich acid soil these increase quickly and build up into broad groups, producing masses of flowers during June and early July, after most of the rhododendrons and azaleas are over – I like to grow them as foreground to these, or associating with groups of meconopsis. The yellow *I. innominata* forms look splendid in front of the blue meconopsis, *M. grandis* and *M. betonicifolia*, and the lavender blue shades in front of the spectacular large rosettes and the tall flower spikes of *M. napaulensis* in its pink and red shades.

There are several very beautiful small species, which I prefer to associate with other alpines in the rock garden or peat bed as they are much less robust than the Californians and need similar conditions. The smallest are *I. lacustris* and the very similar *I. cristata*, which make mats of rhizomes with 1–2 in (2.5–5 cm) long leaves and in May bear dainty flowers, one or two to a stem, pale lavender blue with white and yellow markings. In *Iris gracilipes* the flowers are of a similar flat-topped shape but the stems are considerably longer – up to 10 in (25 cm). Although it is taller, it is not a very vigorous plant and I think the rock garden is the best place for it.

MIMULUS

This genus presents a striking contrast to most of the shade-lovers previously mentioned with their delicacy of leaf and subdued charm. Here, we generally

Figure 23   Iris cristata

have very vivid colours which need careful placing in such select company. I must confess to an active dislike of some of the brightly spotted large-flowered hybrids, which remind me of the more bloated calceolarias. This is therefore a very personal choice and several of the more colourful varieties can be found in catalogues, for those who like them. Having said that the colours are often somewhat harsh, I have found two mimulus which make good low carpets suitable for any company! These are 'Andean Nymph', which, as the name suggests, was collected in the Andes and is possibly an unnamed species, and the hybrid 'Highland Cream'. 'Andean Nymph' has pale pink flowers tinged with yellow, a delightful soft colour. 'Highland Cream' is a beautiful soft pale yellow – an excellent colour to associate with the blues of larger plants. I find all the mimulus short-lived, or maybe they are not quite fully hardy. It is always as well to keep a few cuttings rooted and to split up and move the plants when they start looking untidy or unhappy. *Mimulus primuloides* is the smallest of them all: a ground-hugging mat with short stems of small bright yellow flowers. Although quite easy in moist soil, its small size makes it more suitable for the peat garden.

Of the unspotted but brightly-coloured varieties, 'Whitecroft Scarlet' and 'Highland Red' are two of the best, very similar with a mass of pale green leaves overtopped with brilliant red flowers, one or two to a stem.

All these mimulus like moisture and, in really boggy conditions, they are happy in full sun. Unless you have a bog garden it is simpler to grow them in semi-shade in humus-rich conditions, in the same way as the equally bog-loving candelabra primulas. In my own garden, with no natural water, I have to rely on watering and humus to enable me to grow these plants, and they seem to do well enough to be worth while, even if I cannot emulate the wonderful displays possible in damp woodland.

OURISIA

Back to a genus of more subtle charms! Most of the ourisias are mat-formers with creeping rhizomes just below the soil surface. They are all attractive in leaf as well as in flower and for the most part are not difficult in woodland conditions. The largest, and possibly the best for general garden use, is *Ourisia macrophylla*, which can spread its rhizomes quite widely and has large-toothed leathery leaves and spikes of pure white flowers in whorls up the stem. In my experience it needs rich soil to show its full beauty. I find that for a couple of years after planting it produces plenty of leaves and two or three whorls of flowers to each stem, then the rhizomes become increasingly bare of leaves and it confines itself to a single whorl of flowers. That is the time to dig it up and replant healthy portions of it into fresh well-prepared soil. Other species seem to behave in the same way on a smaller scale. The South American *Ourisia coccinea* spreads almost too freely in ideal conditions, but has never been a menace here in a low-rainfall area. It is unusual in having brilliant scarlet flowers, not always very freely produced, and has given rise to a beautiful hybrid with pale pink flowers, 'Loch Ewe', an excellent plant if treated in the same way as *O. macrophylla*. One of my favourites is the much smaller ourisia, 'Snowflake', which spreads gradually, making a low carpet of small-toothed leaves above which the 2 in (5 cm) stems carry solitary or, occasionally, a pair of attractive white flowers. This is definitely a mini-carpeter for well-prepared well-drained soil. *O. caespitosa* and its variety *gracilis* are even smaller, making ground-hugging mats of tiny leaves and having very small short-stemmed white flowers.

PHLOX

In Chapter 2, I enthused about the numerous sun-loving dwarf phlox as first-class easy alpines. In addition to these there are several species, and hybrids from them, which seem to be less well-known in gardens and yet are among the very best 'carpeters', which are easy to grow and will cover plenty of ground when established, to a height usually of about 6–8 in (15–20 cm). They are among my favourite plants for ground-cover among shrubs or along the front of mixed borders.

The most important shade-loving species are *Phlox adsurgens*, *P. divaricata*, *P. procumbens* and *P. stolonifera*, but there are several named varieties of doubtful origin – doubtful as far as the catalogues offering them are concerned – which originated as selected clones or hybrids of these.

Phlox adsurgens seems to me the least robust of these shade-loving species but is the most beautifully coloured, with flowers of a soft salmon pink. In good humus-rich but reasonably well-drained soil it will make a spreading carpet of glossy leaves with short stems of several flowers during May and June. In the best forms the flowers are well rounded with overlapping petals. There is a named clone, 'Wagon Wheels', which I would have been inclined to strangle at birth, as it has very narrow-petalled starry flowers of admittedly similar colour!

The most vigorous and far-spreading of these phlox are forms of *P. stolonifera*, with prostrate stems which root freely at the nodes. The upright flower stems are about 6 in (15 cm) high, and carry round trusses of large flowers, which are deep pink in the type plant and in the clone 'Pink Ridge', pale lavender blue in 'Blue Ridge', and pure white in 'Ariane'. The only fault of these excellent plants is that they exhaust the soil, at least in my garden, and although they continue to act as ground-cover, their flowering becomes increasingly sparse. You must either be content with few flowers or move a few rooted pieces to pastures new every two or three years.

Another excellent species of similar size and habit, but not rooting down in the same way, is *P. divaricata*, making a tangled mass of semi-prostrate stems with pale green leaves and smothering itself regularly with flowers, several to a stem, in late spring and early summer. The variety usually offered is 'Laphamii' which has beautiful pale blue flowers, and another recently offered is 'Dirigo Ice', with off-white flowers just tinged with palest violet.

Phlox 'Millstream' is a fairly recently introduced hybrid, probably derived from *Phlox procumbens*, itself a hybrid of *P. stolonifera*. It is a rather more compact plant with similar trusses of flowers, which are deep purplish-pink with a darker eye, a beautiful introduction named after the fine garden in the Eastern USA where it arose.

The most dramatic of all these plants is phlox 'Chattahoochee', which is probably a hybrid between *P. divaricata* and the taller shade-loving *Phlox pilosa*, a superb long-flowering pale pink species. 'Chattahoochee' builds up into a mound of dark prostrate stems of deep green leaves, completely covered during early summer with deep lavender flowers with a striking reddish-purple eye. I have had difficulty finding the best position for it, but it is now flourishing in rich well-drained soil where it only gets full sun for two or three hours in the middle of the day. It seems to need some sun but, in the south, resents full exposure.

POLYGONATUM

The Solomon's seals are among the most beautiful large woodland plants with their arching stems and dangling green and white narrow bell flowers, and they include some of the most striking of variegated plants. They are mainly too tall for our consideration and are often excessively vigorous, but among them are a few dainty species small enough for the rock garden, although they tend to run underground and are safer among shrubs or with other small shade-lovers in a mixed border.

White is not the only colour found in the genus: *Polygonatum hookeri*, the smallest of all, has almost stemless pink flowers with widely spreading petals – not the typical flower shape. It spreads slowly by underground rhizomes and has small leaves only an inch or so high.

Polygonatum humile (*P. falcatum* of gardens) is possibly the smallest of the white-flowered species, again with spreading rhizomes, but with 3–6 in (8–15 cm) upright stems with sessile leaves and greenish-white flowers dangling from the leaf axils, a dainty plant which never gets out of hand in my garden. *P. falcatum* is taller and has an excellent variegated form.

Most of the other species are too tall, but *P. stewartianum* only seems to reach about a foot high here in the south and increases slowly, with whorls of very narrow deep pinkish-purple flowers in early summer.

POLYGONUM

This large genus contains a number of quite rampant carpeters for sun or partial shade, which have been mentioned in Chapter 2. My one favourite in a generally rather boring (to me!) genus is *Polygonum tenuicaule*, a very neat slow-growing species only an inch or two high with tiny dark green leaves and short spikes of white flowers in spring – not really a carpeter except on the smallest scale, and well-worth growing in the rock garden in a choice place.

SAXIFRAGA

We have looked at many sections of this huge genus, but there are some 'odds and ends' left, which are worth mentioning. The 'Fortunei' group I will mention later, and the important 'Mossy' group I have described briefly in the early season section (see p. 70), although they flower well into the mid-season period.

The most important group otherwise is that containing 'London pride' – *Saxifraga × urbium*. This is too well-known to describe here, but it is not very tall and is useful in poor shady conditions. There is a variegated form of it with yellow blotches on the leaves, which may have added appeal for some! Its real importance to the alpine enthusiast is that it has given rise to one or two very pleasing miniatures under the name *S. × urbium primuloides*, notably 'Ingwersen's Variety' and 'Elliott's Variety', commemorating two of the greatest alpine 'names' of the past fifty years. They are probably identical, miniatures of London Pride with rounded rosettes of toothed leaves and spikes of dainty pink flowers, very easily grown and an excellent edging to a shady border.

Figure 24   Polygonum tenuicaule

Smaller than these is my favourite of the group, *Saxifraga × primulaize* and its variety 'Salmon', with neat rosettes and short sprays of deep red or salmon flowers. It can be grown on the flat, but is especially effective in the interstices of a north-facing wall.

STYLOPHORUM AND OTHERS
Somehow we tend to associate poppy flowers with the sun, and it may be a surprise to know that there are several genera of the poppy family that revel in shady conditions, *Stylophorum* being one of the best known, together with *Hylomecon*, *Eomecon* and, of course, *Meconopsis*, which can hardly be included among carpeters, unless you are unfortunate enough to grow *Meconopsis cambrica*, the 'Welsh poppy', a deep-rooting free-seeding menace in sun or in shade.

The problems of growing meconopsis will be dealt with later (see p. 103) – there is really no excuse for including them in this book, except that they are alpine in nature and loved by all alpine growers! These other poppies are all easy and perennial, capable of spreading into quite broad clumps. *Eomecon chionantha*, in fact, needs careful placing as its roots spread widely in optimum conditions. It is probably as well to starve it a little, or you may regret its excessive spread, however much you enjoy its fine white flowers on 18 in (45 cm) stems. It needs large shrubs for company.

Hylomecon japonicum is a more restrained plant with attractive pinnate leaves and bright yellow poppies on 8–12 in (20–30 cm) stems, which never seem to get out of hand in my garden. The stylophorums are similar, but they form rather taller, more robust clumps of deeply-cut leaves, with a long succession of yellow flowers throughout the summer. The species generally grown is *S. diphyllum*, but I have recently acquired *S. lasiocarpum*, which seems to me to have more beautiful leaves, deeply-cut and of an unusually pale yellowish-green colour, with an endless succession of flowers all through the summer.

VIOLAS

These are discussed in detail among the sun-lovers (see p. 39), but it must be said that most of them do as well, or better, in partial shade. In several parts of the garden I grow *Viola cornuta* and its white form among taller perennials and larger shrubs, where they are considerably overshadowed. Like some of the spreading geraniums they have a delightful habit of climbing up among the branches of, for example, shrub roses, helping to clothe their usual nakedness just above the ground. Two species that I failed to mention earlier, because they have a definite preference for shade, are *Viola biflora* and *Viola papilionacea*, with which I include *V. cucullata*.

Viola biflora is a charming little species with pale green rounded leaves and short stems carrying one or (more often) two typical viola flowers, which are bright yellow with brownish stripes at the throat. It is small enough for the peat bed but will spread around happily among shrubs.

I grow a delightful viola under the name *V. papilionacea* var. *priceana*, which has white flowers with a dark violet-blue centre. It is much stronger-growing than *V. biflora* and so can be used among more robust neighbours. The name is the problem, because I have seen very similar plants offered as *V. papilionacea* and also as *V. cucullata*. I think the first name is correct, as a monograph describes the two latter species (which incidentally are very similar) as blue, but says they also have less obviously marked albinos. Whatever the name – I suggest you see it in flower – it is a good easy shade-lover for every garden.

Main Alpines for Mid-season

As in Chapter 2, I propose to describe here some of the finest alpines that flower between May and August, but that will thrive in shady conditions as long as the soil preparation has been adequate. Some of the bulbs described for early season will probably go on flowering into May, especially the trilliums, and there are orchids and aroids to follow these, which I shall deal with first.

AROIDS

Most of the true arums are sun-lovers, but the beautiful *Arum creticum* seems to grow equally well here in the shade of trees. It resembles our native 'lords and ladies', but has a beautiful clear yellow spathe. If arums are among your

95

unfavourite weeds, as they are in my garden, great care is needed to avoid digging up your *Arum creticum* in mistake for a native, as the leaves are similar! *Arum italicum* var. *pictum* gives good foliage for flower arrangements but is really too robust to be considered alpine.

Arisarum proboscoideum is the only member of its genus commonly culti-vated and is well worth while, if only to amuse the children. It forms a low carpet of small arrow-shaped leaves about 2–3 in (5–8 cm) high. The mouse-sized spathes are dark brown with white underneath, and have long tails, so that they look exactly like mice disappearing into the foliage. It is very easily grown and spreads quite widely – in fact, it could well have been included among the carpeters.

The most important aroid genus is *Arisaema*, which seems to invoke a love–hate relationship in alpine gardeners, who are almost equally divided between those who find it fascinating and those who find it ugly. There is a reasonable number of species available to the enthusiast, and most do well in rich soil in shady or semi-shady conditions. I shall confine myself to a few of the more spectacular, and refer anyone truly 'bitten' by them to more specialised literature.

By far the most popular, and certainly the most attractively coloured, is *Arisaema candidissimum*, with 4 in (10 cm) pink spathes with longitudinal white stripes. Beware of its one fault – the flowers and large leaves do not appear until late May and it is all too easy to plant something else on top of it during the spring planting season! In my garden it is growing at the edge of a peat bed sheltered by a wall, so that it is only in the sun at the height of summer, but this seems to suit it well and I suspect it would be quite happy in full sun.

Arisaema flavum is a delightful species with smaller bright yellow spathes, which seems quite hardy. One of the most dramatic species is *A. sikokianum*, which has a deep purple spathe, green within, and a conspicuous white spadix expanded towards the tip. So far in my limited experience it has proved hardy.

One of the hardiest of all is the American 'jack-in-the-pulpit', *Arisaema triphyllum*, with a green spathe of medium size, striped lengthwise with white or paler green, a beautiful peat-bed plant.

ORCHIDS

The hardy terrestrial orchids are a fascinating group, which I hesitate to recommend because only the dactylorrhizas increase freely in cultivation and can be acquired as homegrown stock. The cypripediums are among the most beautiful woodland or peat-bed plants, and there are few finer sights than the established clumps to be seen in the Savill Gardens, at Wisley and in a few other gardens. They are occasionally offered by nurseries, but until we can be sure that they did not originate from stock lifted in the wild, I think they should be avoided. I hope that they will soon be available from micro-propagation, and we will be able to grow them with a clear conscience. The same strictures probably apply to the calanthes, which in general seem also to be more tender than cypripediums.

Figure 25   Arisaema candidissima

The dactylorrhizas are among my favourite shade-loving perennials, with a very long flowering season around midsummer. I find that they increase freely, doubling at least each season. The two usually available are very similar, *Dactylorrhiza foliosa* (*D. maderensis*) and *D. elata*. Seen side by side, *D. elata* seems to be a little taller, with a longer and marginally paler spike of deep reddish-purple flowers, and with bracts protruding between the flowers. *D. foliosa*, for me, certainly increases much more freely, and I have been able to plant several good clumps around the garden, to flower with the later primulas and meconopsis. As long as the site is always reasonably moist it will tolerate quite a lot of sun here in the south, and doubtless full sun in the wetter counties. These species have unspotted leaves, but there is a dactylorrhiza in gardens with similar flowers and leaves heavily spotted dark brown, possibly *Dactylor-rhiza* × *grandis*. The smaller-flowered and paler *D. maculata* is also offered occasionally, and I find that it increases freely in the garden.

The only other orchids readily available are *Bletilla striata*, *Epipactis gigantea* and the pleiones. The *Bletilla* is frequently offered and yet I cannot succeed with it. It is a beautiful plant with large rose-coloured flowers on 6–8 in (15–20 cm) stems, which should be happy in humus-rich soil in partial shade, but all my efforts to grow it have failed – I am still trying! *Epipactis gigantea*, on the other hand, is a devastating success, which has taken over a couple of yards of peat bed and is now establishing itself in the gravel path alongside – imagine an orchidaceous weed! It is quite attractive with its small flowers, very similar to our native marsh helleborine, a strange mixture of red and yellow. I suspect that it would be more restrained in a heavier soil.

Although I would never look upon pleiones as garden plants, they can be managed with some sort of overhead winter protection, and I think they are among the most superb plants for the cold greenhouse, their beauty an eye-opener to any gardener unfamiliar with them. They are magnificently exhibited at Chelsea and at Vincent Square, so that few can have failed to see them, but let me say here that, in spite of their beauty, their basic requirements are easily fulfilled. They do not need an orchid compost, but a mixture, say, of loam, peat and leaf-mould with plenty of added grit, dry conditions in winter and abundant water in spring and early summer. They all have large flowers on quite short rigid stems arising from the bases of their curious green pseudo-bulbs. Most of the species have been lumped under *Pleione bulbocodioides*, but they may still be found under their original names, *P. formosanum* and *P. pricei*, or various clonal names, which cover a range of colour from white to deep rosey-purple, usually with a pale lip heavily marked with purple spots and lines, or, in the case of the albinos, with yellow. *P. pogonioides* and *P. yunnanense* have particularly dark flowers, and *P. humilis* has much smaller off-white flowers with brownish markings on the lips. *P. limprichtii* is another especially good and hardy species with small deep purple flowers.

There is one superb yellow-flowered species, generally but apparently incorrectly known as *P. forrestii*, the large flowers identical in form to those of *P. bulbocodioides*, but of a beautiful clear yellow with reddish markings on the lip.

ANEMONOPSIS MACROPHYLLA

Leaving the bulbs, this is one of the many Japanese woodland plants with a special beauty that is hard to analyse. It is about 12–18 in (30–45 cm) high when its large anemone-like leaves are fully developed, and the branching flower spikes rise well above them, so that it may be a little large for the smaller rock garden or the peat bed, although conditions there are ideal for it – moist and humus-rich. Here I grow it under a *Styrax japonica* in what was originally a rich moist peat bed, but is now becoming increasingly overhung and filled with roots. For about ten years the *Anemonopsis* has flourished, but now the competition is becoming too much and I must move it to another shady spot. Its flowers resemble semi-double miniatures of *Anemone japonica*, dangling upside-down, several to a stem, intriguingly coloured deep purplish-violet outside and paling almost to white within. Although never spectacular it has a reasonably long flowering period, and visitors to the garden always admire its quiet beauty.

BULBINELLA

This is another genus with only one species readily available, *B. hookeri*, an excellent easily-grown plant for semi-shade with some moisture. It has very much the habit of a miniature kniphofia, with a rosette of narrow yellowish-green leaves often tinged with bronze, and narrow golden-yellow 'pokers' up to 8 in (20 cm) in height. It is easily raised from seed, although I have never noticed it seeding itself, so that a group of several plants together can be planted in a shady border, or singly in a collection of other alpines.

CALCEOLARIA

A name likely to evoke shudders in the alpine enthusiasts, but although so many of the large species are the antithesis of alpines, blowsy and garish, there are in fact several delightful miniatures, including some to test the expert's skill. These latter treasures are *Calceolaria darwinii* and *C. fothergillii* and the recent hybrid between them 'Walter Shrimpton'. They are usually seen in the alpine house, but in my experience they are not too difficult in rich scree conditions, preferably in a raised bed with some winter protection, in sun or partial shade. From a cluster of dark green hairy leaves, which are the favourite diet of every slug around, arise 3 in (8 cm) stems each bearing an incredible flower, which is dark yellow behind with a brown face with a pure white band across it. This really describes *C. darwinii*; *C. fothergillii* has smaller, narrower and less strikingly-marked flowers. The hybrid is almost as spectacular as *C. darwinii* and considerably easier to grow. Whichever you choose, propagate them by seed (the species), or by cuttings, as they are always short-lived and very liable to red spider under glass.

The other small species are less exciting but much easier to grow. My favourite is the tiny *Calceolaria tenella*, which creeps over the surface of the ground, making a carpet of miniscule leaves on which the small yellow flowers appear on slender one inch (2.5 cm) stems. *C. polyrhiza* and *C. acutifolia* are considerably larger, perhaps 6–8 in (15–20 cm) in flower, with larger pouched yellow flowers generally marked with red spots. The widely available calceolaria variety 'John Innes' is a similar low carpeting plant but the flowers are somewhat larger. *C. biflora* is yet another of similar height, generally with the flowers in pairs.

Any of these calceolarias are suitable for a shady place in the rock garden or between low-growing shrubs, as long as they have abundant moisture and humus.

Figure 26   Clintonia andrewsiana

CLINTONIA

A small but rarely-grown genus of intriguing woodlanders, not likely to win prizes for flower power but fascinating none the less. One of my favourite peat-bed plants has always been *Clintonia andrewsiana*, the only species with flowers other than white. It has rosettes of broad glossy green leaves only a few inches high, with 10 in (25 cm) stems bearing heads of small deep rose flowers, which are followed a month or two later by deep violet-blue berries which last well on the plant and do not seem popular with birds. That is to say, I usually win the race when looking for seed!

Among the white-flowered species I think *C. umbellata* is the most satisfactory. It has increased well in a peat bed, with similar but smaller broad leaves and short stems carrying umbels of little pure white flowers, followed by rather inconspicuous black fruits. *Clintonia uniflora* and the closely allied *C. udensis* are similar, but they have only one or two flowers per stem, which seem to be very fleeting (I often miss them!), followed again by dark berries which at least stay on the plant for some time.

CODONOPSIS

This is another intriguing genus, containing several low climbers and a few upright-growing plants towards the upper size limit for this book. It also contains one or two menaces! After some ten years I am still pulling out evil-smelling stems and roots of a plant whose name is long forgotten, but which spread over the years through most of a 30 ft (9m) long peat bed. It 'climbs' rather faster beneath the ground than above, where it is a low scrambler with strange greenish heavily streaked bell flowers. Beware the species with the most subdued colouring!

Although climbers are not often included among alpines, the genus *Codonopsis* contains two most beautiful plants not to be missed. Perhaps I should mention their one major fault first: their growth starts as a very thin fragile shoot which, if broken during enthusiastic weeding, seems incapable of regeneration. I keep doing it! You can, of course, grow them in pots under glass, perhaps up short pea sticks or a similar contrivance, where they will be safe, or you can try like me to let them scramble through low shrubs, preferably with a large notice saying 'do not weed here'!

The first of these climbers is *C. convolvulacea*, which can attain 3–4 ft (90–120 cm). It has sparsely-leaved stems and astonishingly large pale blue open bell-shaped flowers with purple centres. It also has a wonderful pure white-flowered form 'Alba' which thrills me whenever I see it. *C. vincaeflora* is similar but less robust, with pure blue flowers of similar shape.

The commonest of the upright-growing species is *C. mollis*, with hairy greyish leaves and pale blue dangling bells with darker markings within. *C. ovata* has more prostrate stems and the flowers have a purple basal blotch. *C. clematidea* is somewhat similar with even longer stems of pale blue bells. In *C. meleagris* the flowers are not blue but greenish, with conspicuous yellow and brown markings inside the bells.

DIGITALIS

It seems quite a jump from the mainly Asiatic exotic codonopsis to the more humdrum, generally European, foxgloves. Here again we are on the border-line for size, but several foxgloves keep below 18 in (45 cm) and are very easy to grow. They look best in groups of at least three and preferably more, depending on the space available, among larger perennials or shrubs. They are very easy to grow from seed, so that raising enough for large groups should not be a problem, except that your favourite *Digitalis dubia* or your *Digitalis heywoodii* may have become *D. vulgaris* when they eventually flower! They have terrible morals! However hard I try to weed out all my vulgar foxgloves, seed rarely comes true from these two favourites – my bees evidently travel a long way as I am sure my only near neighbour has no foxgloves.

Having started with their one fault, I should say that the two species mentioned both have fine silvery leaves, much more striking than those of the common foxglove, and they would be worth growing just for their foliage. *D. dubia* has beautiful 12 in (30 cm) spikes of pale pink flowers (very like foxgloves!) and *D. heywoodii*, probably a subspecies of *D. vulgaris*, has even whiter leaves and slightly taller spikes of white flowers, sometimes with the faintest tinge of pink.

Most of the others are better behaved. *D ferruginea* has glossy green rosettes and strange dense spikes of dark brown flowers – sombre but quite effective in a group, especially if you can find a light background like a white-variegated elaeagnus. *D. lanata* is taller with a looser spike of flowers, which are a combination of brown and yellow, varying in different forms. In *D. lutea* the flowers are smaller again and pure creamy yellow. My favourite yellow species is *D. grandiflora*, a taller plant with flowers almost as big as ordinary foxgloves, again of a pleasing soft colour. All these are perennial and seed themselves around, brightening up the darker corners of a shady border.

Digitalis obscura is special – a shrubby sun-loving species from Spain with reddish flowers. It has been reintroduced quite recently, but it is undoubtedly tricky, hence the need for the reintroduction I suppose. In spite of its natural habitat I have found it most successful with a little shade, but even then it does not regularly survive the winter. It is semi-shrubby to about 10–12 in (25–30 cm), with dark green leaves and short spikes of deep yellow flowers heavily suffused with red, especially in some forms. It sets a little seed and I have also found it quite easy to propagate from cuttings.

DODECATHEON

Dodecatheons are closely allied to primulas, but have flowers of an unusual shape, with reflexed petals and a prominent proboscis of stigma and stamens, which has given rise to their common name of 'shooting stars'. There are a number of different species and their varying requirements need careful study to achieve perfection, but here I propose to oversimplify by saying that they enjoy the same conditions as the moisture-loving primulas to be discussed later. A few like full sun and drying off in summer, but I will confine myself here to the easier ones.

All have rosettes of smooth glossy, more or less untoothed leaves, differing in fact from most primulas and varying only in size. They bear several nodding shooting-star flowers to a stem, varying in colour from white, through shades of pink, to the darkest purplish magenta. I grow them in the peat bed, where they follow the erythroniums and trilliums, in groups between such tall ericaceous shrubs as *Leiophyllum buxifolium*, cassiopes and phyllodoces. The larger species can equally well be grown among taller shrubs in the front of the border, as long as they get plenty of moisture in spring.

Dodecatheon meadia is one of the commonest and easiest with 12 in (30 cm) stems carrying umbels of deep rose flowers, pale towards the base with orange anthers. *D. jeffreyi* is similar, with dark anthers. One of my favourites of the reddish-flowered species is *D. pulchellum* 'Red Wings', with deep crimson flowers, perhaps the most striking of them all. One or two species have white flowers, which show up well against the sombre dark green of evergreen shrubs. Unfortunately, I find them less easy to satisfy because they prefer drier conditions and a little more sun. There is a white form of *D. meadia*, which should be as easy as the type, but the most commonly available is *D. dentatum*, the whiteness of its flowers contrasting with its prominent, almost black anthers.

INCARVILLEA

It seems curious that the incarvilleas are not more popular, as they have spectacularly large flowers reminiscent of those of the fat greenhouse gloxinias, and yet are reasonably easy in a moist rich soil, preferably in partial shade in the south, but happy in full sun further north. Some of the species are a little tall, and I shall confine myself to those unlikely to attain much more than 1 ft (30 cm) in height.

Incarvillea delavayi is definitely too tall, although highly to be recommended, but the other species most often offered in catalogues, *I. mairei*, is generally under 18 in (45 cm) and has several dwarfer named varieties, such as 'Nyoto Sama' and 'Frank Ludlow', as well as the more robust 'Bees Pink'. I like these dwarfs and I only wish they would increase more freely. Their large pink trumpets on stiff 4–12 in (10–30 cm) stems appear in early summer from rosettes of crinkly bluish-green leaves and can combine strikingly with the larger 'dwarf' rhododendrons, especially those with white, cream or blue flowers, or with patches of the blue Pacific Coast irises such as *Iris douglasiana*.

Recently, new species of *Incarvillea* have appeared on the garden scene, notably *I. olgae* and *I. arguta*. These are very similar to each other, forming a tangle of semi-prostrate stems with small leaves, among which the flowers appear on short stalks. Both have good clear pink flowers but these are much narrower and more delicate in form, and appear much later than those of *I. mairei* or *I. delvayi*.

LEWISIAS

Lewisias have already been described as sun-lovers (see p. 50), but I cannot resist recommending them again as I find that they definitely flourish better in semi-shady conditions in Kent, especially when planted on their sides in walls facing away from the sun. They are such beautiful plants that it is worth experimenting with different positions in really well-drained soil in the rock garden, raised bed or trough.

MECONOPSIS

I suppose I am cheating here, but every alpine enthusiast reads about meconopsis growing in the Himalayas among the true alpines, and wants to grow

103

them somewhere in the garden! They are far too tall for the rock garden, but are wonderful in woodland conditions, even if you are restricted to a few square feet among tall shrubs. One of the most beautiful sights of the summer garden is a group of meconopsis growing with moisture-loving primulas, which flower at the same time.

As far as the most important species are concerned – the real 'blue poppies', *Meconopsis grandis*, with its several named clones, and *M. betonicifolia* – I shall confine myself to a few words about cultivation. In Scotland I think you can almost plant them and forget them, but the further south and the further east you progress the more difficult they become. However, you can grow them even in Kent, and in some gardens like Sandling Park you could believe yourself in a Scottish dell, where they have natural moist woodland. In an ordinary garden you need to dig in lots of well-rotted manure, compost, leaf-mould or peat, and in summer you must keep them watered. The same applies, of course, to the much larger monocarpic species such as *M. napaulensis* and *M. paniculata* with their glorious gold or silver-haired rosettes, followed (unfortunately!) by 6 ft (1.8 m) spires of small poppies in shades of pink, purple or yellow.

The one reliably perennial dwarf meconopsis is the 'harebell poppy', *M. quintuplinervia*, which is quite different from the other species in making a spreading mat of small hairy rosettes of grey-green leaves up to 6 in (15 cm), above which rise upright stems each bearing a large pale blue pendant bell. This is a most beautiful plant, needing really good conditions to succeed. I find it exhausts its original soil and needs splitting every two or three years and replanting in freshly prepared ground.

One or two species small enough to be regarded as dwarfs are, alas, monocarpic. Fortunately, they are also easily raised from seed. The obvious choice is *M. horridula*, a fascinating plant covered with brownish hairs – one might almost call them bristles – and producing, after one or two years, a spike up to a foot high of large greyish-blue flowers. The colour varies but I find it is not usually poor enough to be 'wishy-washy'. The other monocarpic species, a little larger, which I would recommend is *M. dhwojii*. In rich soil this can become rather large before dying after flowering. It is another very hairy plant, with abundant bronze hairs which make a delightful background to the pale yellow flowers.

One of my favourite monocarpic species near to our size limit is *M. latifolia*. I rarely see this in other gardens, although its hairy leaves are attractive and its upright stems are well-furnished with flowers of a particularly beautiful shade of pale blue. I have not seen much variation in this colour, but maybe I have been lucky!

PRIMULA

During the summer months an entirely different group of primulas comes into its own. Generally classed as 'bog primulas', they belong mostly to the Candelabra section with whorls of flowers up their stems in a galaxy of colours.

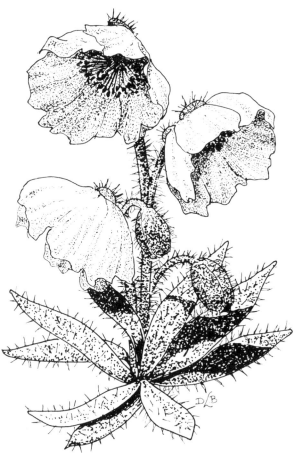

Figure 27   Meconopsis horridula

In addition to these, there are a few other species which flower late in the season and generally enjoy similar, but perhaps not quite such wet conditions.

The candelabra primulas, together with *P. florindae* and *P. sikkimensis*, are the easiest of plants if you are fortunate enough to have natural moisture in the garden. Not far from my own garden there is a superb example of their use at Sandling Park, near Hythe. Although rhododendrons and other fine trees and shrubs predominate there, the garden is transformed towards the end of their flowering season by the great drifts of primulas, which flourish exceedingly and seed themselves prodigiously in the constantly wet woodland conditions, accompanied by fine meconopsis.

Few gardens possess this idyllic combination of moisture and humus beneath a canopy of well-spaced tall trees, but it is still possible to grow these primulas with some special preparation. In my own garden there is no natural moisture but plenty of shade from trees and from walls, and I find the secret of success, as with the meconopsis, is the incorporation of plenty of manure and peat, and watering during dry spells. Remember that the more thorough the preparation the less watering will be required, and it is only in the driest counties – like Kent – that it will be necessary with any frequency.

A considerable number of different bog primulas is available from nursery catalogues and they are all worth growing, including some of the strains of mixed colours like the 'Inshriach Strain'. Try to see them at shows and in gardens, to choose your favourite colours, but I will recommend a few which appeal to me most.

Primula helodoxa is probably the easiest of the yellow-flowered species, a robust plant with several whorls to a stem. In *P. aurantiaca* and *P. bulleyana* the colour deepens to orange. In this colour range I like the diminutive *P. cockburniana* with little bright orange flowers on 6 in (15 cm) stems. Unfortunately it is short-lived, and you must keep growing a few from seed.

Primula pulverulenta is an outstanding species with splendid spikes of deep purple-red flowers. The stems are covered with white farina and this added feature makes it, for me, the best in this colour. The 'Bartley Strain' is derived from this species and widens the colour range in the pinks to purples. *P. japonica* is perhaps the best-known of all the Candelabra section, again with deep-reddish flowers, and is also the parent of 'Postford White'. I have always had a particular liking for white flowers, and if I could only grow one moisture-loving primula this would undoubtedly be my choice. It has the typical whorls of flowers but they are pure white with yellow centres, and they are marvellous for brightening up shady corners. They seem to come true from self-sown seed, and I find I am gradually acquiring an ever-increasing drift of them in the shade of an old apple tree, growing with some *Meconopsis betonicaefolia* and *Cardiocrinum giganteum*, which enjoy the same generous soil preparation.

Although I always prefer groups of single species of uniform colour in my own garden, I frequently admire drifts of some of the fine mixed strains available, for example the 'Bartley Strain', mainly pale pink through to deep purple, and the 'Inshriach' and 'Bressingham Strains', in which yellow has been incorporated, so that you have a beautiful picture of soft pinks and yellows and shades between.

Apart from those described, there are several other Asiatic primulas which will thrive in the same conditions. *Primula florindae* is like a massive cowslip with large rounded heads of pale yellow flowers, up to a metre high in wet soil. I fear this is one species which should be left to gardeners in naturally wet areas, unless you are prepared to do a lot of watering! On the other hand *P. sikkimensis* is more adaptable, and it gives the same effect on a smaller scale, with similar cream-coloured flowers. One of my favourites in this group is *P. secundiflora*, with flower heads of a rich deep reddish-purple. I find it very easy to grow from seed and it flourishes in the company of my 'Postford White'.

Most of the species mentioned so far have been robust plants which look best in massed groups, but there are others which have a special appeal as more typical alpines for the peat bed or shady area of the rock garden. *P. capitata* and its subspecies *mooreana* are very late-flowering dainty species with clusters of small deep bluish-purple flowers, resembling miniatures of *P. denticulata*. Like so many of the smaller Asiatic primulas I find them short-lived but easily raised from seed.

Perhaps the most remarkable of all these primulas is *P. vialii*, which I fell in love with many years ago and have endeavoured to keep going in the garden ever since. Seeing it out of flower one would have no inkling that the spikes would be unusual, but when they appear in June they resemble miniature 'red hot pokers', with brilliant crimson unopened buds above and a dense column of lavender flowers opening beneath. Few plants evoke more interest from visitors, and yet with a little determination a group of them can be maintained fairly easily. As with *Meconopsis betonicifolia*, the flowering rosette itself dies, so that, unless it has built up a cluster of rosettes, the plant will die. The better the soil the more likely you are to have perennial plants, but in any case it is well to treat it as a biennial and sow a little seed each year. It always sets plenty!

THALICTRUM
Most of the thalictrums, beautiful though they are, are too tall to be considered here, but one at least is an outstanding small plant for a shady place. This is *Thalictrum kiusianum*, a dainty little species with attractive ferny leaves and short stems (6 in (15 cm) or less) of fluffy pale purple flowers. Given a light peaty soil it runs gently underground, but it is so small that I like to grow it in a prominent place in the peat bed or foreground of the rock garden. It is another wonderful example of the beauty of Japanese woodland plants.

Thalictrum coreanum is occasionally offered. It is somewhat similar to *T. kiusianum* but at least twice its size, and does not have quite the same beauty.

UVULARIA
A small genus of three woodland species which are a little tall for the rock garden but are ideal if placed in groups among taller shrubs. They are somewhat similar to the Solomon's seals, with tall stems of pale green leaves beneath which hang long narrow yellow bells. *Uvularia grandiflora* is the largest and most readily available, with rather darker yellow flowers than *U. perfoliata*, and taller stems.

I find that uvularias grow satisfactorily even in quite deep shade as long as the soil has been well-prepared with plenty of humus, enjoying the same conditions as the meconopsis, which start flowering later.

Shrubs
I described many of the shrubs flowering in shady conditions in the previous 'early season' section, including a selection of rhododendrons, many of which could well have been included here, as their season can continue as late as July. There are a few other predominantly ericaceous shrubs which start flowering during this season and which need the same conditions – an acid soil with peat and leaf-mould.

107

Figure 28   Thalictrum kiusianum

The kalmias are all likely to become too large eventually to be considered as alpines, but two of the smaller-flowered species are slow-growing and take several years to achieve a height of 2 ft (60 cm). These are *Kalmia angustifolia* and *K. polifolia*, which I find grow and flower best if they can have sunshine for at least part of the day while keeping their roots moist, like their larger relation *K. latifolia* in its galaxy of forms.

Kalmia polifolia in my garden makes a rather sparse upright shrub with small evergreen leaves. The flowers are produced in flat clusters at the tips of the shoots in April, attractively cup-shaped and deep rose in colour. *K. polifolia* var. *microphylla* (*K. microphylla*) is a more compact spreading form, which should keep under a foot high, so that it is more suitable for a choice place.

Kalmia angustifolia seems to me to be very similar in habit, but it flowers much later in June. Both species are sparser in growth than I would like, but both have most beautiful small flowers like miniatures of those of *K. latifolia*, and seem much easier to please in the garden than the latter.

I was in some doubt whether to mention the leucothoes as most of them are too large, although their beautiful spreading arching growth prevents them from getting too tall. I am including them on the strength of the 'Minor' form of *Leucothoe keiskii*, which is a much more compact slow-growing plant with low arching stems of reddish-tinged leaves and little pendant white bells. In ideal peaty conditions I suspect it may run gently, but after growing it for a couple of years I am still awaiting the day!

The menziesias are among my favourite ericaceous shrubs, especially *Menziesia ciliicalyx* var. *purpurea* (*M. lasiophylla*). This is a slow-growing deciduous shrub, very similar in appearance when in leaf to a dwarf rhododendron. The leaves are a beautiful blue colour – in fact, it is worth growing for its foliage alone, but it produces clusters of very attractive nodding bells, pale purple with a grape-like bloom. As it grows in rather deep shade I find it very slow, but it flowers regularly every year in early summer, just as the last trilliums in the same bed are going over.

Figure 29 Uvularia grandiflora

Late Season

Flowering plants

As autumn approaches it becomes more difficult to find flowering plants to brighten the shady areas of the garden, especially if you are precluded from growing the generally lime-hating autumn-flowering gentians. These can be a dramatic feature of any suitable garden; they may even be the highlight of the garden year for anyone specialising in them. On limy soils most gentians are not for you, but just as large colonies of *Cyclamen coum* can be built up to carpet the ground in late winter, so *Cyclamen hederifolium* can be the outstanding spectacle of autumn in any garden and it is easier to produce than the spring picture.

In the earlier section on spring-flowering bulbs I described our one 'mono-typic' bed in the garden, with its splendid display of cyclamen – mainly *C. coum* and *C. hederifolium* (see p. 72). Both species have seeded themselves around very freely with me, but there is no doubt that it is easier to produce carpets of *C. hederifolium* in the autumn than of *C. coum* in the spring. There is not quite the variation in colour in the autumn, as the flowers tend to be either white or pink, but here they have blended into a beautiful patchwork of colour.

Two other autumn-flowering species grow quite well in the open garden, but they have much smaller flowers so I prefer to grow them on the rock garden or in raised beds where they can be enjoyed at close range. These are *Cyclamen cilicium* and *C. intaminatum*. The former generally has marbled leaves and small pale pink flowers. The latter, at one time classified as a subspecies, has delicate little white or palest pink flowers, and rounded deep green leaves in the form grown here.

In previous sections I have described 'easy carpeters' as a separate heading. However, with the more limited choice in autumn, especially of really easy plants, I shall consider all the flowering plants available together, followed by a group of shrubs which are more notable for their fruits than their flowers.

GENTIANS

This is unquestionably the most important genus of alpines at this time of year, except perhaps to the cyclamen enthusiast, and I have described them under the late-flowering sun-lovers (see p. 64). For gardeners in the warmer counties they could have been placed in this section, as they hate dry conditions.

CYANANTHUS

This is a genus of delightful small alpines which, like most of the gentians, needs an acid oil, and I find that they do best in rich scree conditions. There are only a few species in cultivation. They all form a central rootstock from which arise prostrate stems with tiny leaves, on the end of which appear large blue or white saucer-shaped flowers in late summer. The commonest species, which I certainly find the easiest, is *C. lobatus*, which makes a flat carpet of stems about

12 in (30 cm) across and has large deep blue flowers, one to a stem. Catalogues may offer various named varieties of this, which differ in size of flower, the most distinct being the beautful white *C. lobatus* var. *albus. C. microphyllus* (*C. integer*) is similar in habit but is altogether smaller, with tiny leaves on shorter stems and flowers about two-thirds the size of *C. lobatus.*

SAXIFRAGA

Even late in the season this wonderful genus has an important contribution to make in *Saxifraga fortunei* (*S. cortusoides*) and its varieties. What a complete contrast to the spring-flowering species, or even to the later-flowering 'mossies'! *S. fortunei* more closely resembles those other useful shade-lovers of the same family, the heucheras and tiarellas. The typical form makes a clump of large round-lobed leaves up to 10 in (25 cm) high, usually starting green early in the season but becoming increasingly tinged with red towards autumn, when the loose sprays of small white flowers appear on 12 in (30 cm) stems.

During recent years an increasing number of named clones from Japan has become available, varying greatly in size and in the depth of the red or purple tones taken on by the leaves. 'Wada's Form' was among my earliest favourites, one of the larger-growing plants but with excellent red tints. I find it quite robust enough to grow in shady places between rhododendrons to give some late colour after the excitements of the primulas and meconopsis are over. *S. fortunei* 'Rubrifolia' is similar. There are some very neat compact varieties in cultivation now, such as 'Mount Nacki' and 'Rokujo', which do not really have enough impact for a shrub border, and I prefer to grow them in my peat bed or the rock garden, where their beauty can be appreciated with the cyananthus and gentians and other small plants.

TRICYRTIS

Perhaps the common name 'toad lily' reflects the somewhat mixed feelings inspired by this interesting genus. Many of them are a little tall for a book on alpines, but the height varies with growing conditions and they are not often above 2 ft (60 cm) high. They are usually, with one notable exception, very leafy upright plants with their curious-shaped flowers towards the tips of their stems. The flowers have spreading petals and a prominent and rather complicated arrangement of stamens and stigma, all very heavily spotted with darker colouring to give a somewhat sombre effect in the shady conditions they enjoy.

In spite of that lukewarm description I grow as many species as I can find, because I enjoy their unusual flowers, worth studying closely as individuals with their intriguing shapes and abundant spots, and they also come at a time when flowers are few and far between among the shade-lovers. They are too tall for the rock garden, and again I like to grow them between shrubs. As I have said of so many genera, their names seem to be in a muddle, and it is difficult to be sure of getting the species you want unless you see them in flower. The commonest is one of the taller species with deep mauve flowers very heavily spotted with darker colour, most commonly offered as *Tricyrtis*

Figure 30   Tricyrtis macrantha

formosana. This is probably its correct name but it is often confused with *T. hirta*, which should be white with purple spots. One of the most beautiful is *T. hirta* 'Alba' with beautiful unspotted flowers that show up well against a dark background and belie my description of 'sombre'. The same applies to the yellow species *T. latifolia*, probably the same as *T. bakeri*, an upright-growing species with the yellow flowers spotted with purple. The most exciting of all is *T. macrantha* ssp *macanthropsis*, of very different low arching habit with long pendant yellow bell-shaped flowers beneath the leafy stems. I find this grows almost too vigorously in the peat garden, so I have moved it to the foreground

112

of the shrub border. Its one fault with me is that the stems are so low that the flowers are on the ground and easily get spoilt by bad weather. I think it would look marvellous hanging over the edge of a shady wall. *T. macrantha* is more upright-growing with similar yellow flowers.

Fruiting Plants

Berries can play an important part in any garden, and this is as true of small plants on the rock garden as of the larger shrubs in borders. Most of the plants concerned are shrubs, especially Ericaceae, but one or two non-woody plants mentioned previously have a second season of interest: for example, the clintonias, notably *Clintonia andrewsiana* with excellent long-standing blue berries (see p. 100).

Among the shrubs the pernettyas and gaultherias are probably the most important, with a contribution from *Vaccinium* and *Myrtus*. These all require an acid soil, like the other ericaceae described earlier, and they grow best in partial shade in soil enriched with peat or leaf-mould.

Pernettya mucronata is too large to be considered here, though it is a good species for general use, with very large berries in a considerable range of colours, white, pink and deep purple. *Pernettya prostrata* is a more dwarf species, usually grown as its subspecies *pentlandii*. It forms a dense thicket of small-leaved evergreen stems usually less than 1 ft (30 cm) high. The flowers, as in the other species, are insignificant, but in autumn you should get an excellent crop of deep blue berries. A white-fruited form may also be available. I find this very easy to grow, and after a few years it has travelled gradually underground to make a low bush a yard across, but it does not always fruit well, possibly because it is in deep shade. Unlike *P. mucronatum* the flowers are monoecious so it should fruit all by itself!

My favourite species is *P. tasmanica*, a tiny ground-hugging mat, which I grow in the foreground of the peat bed. The flowers contribute little, but every autumn I get a good crop of bright red berries, which are large for the size of the plant and seem to remain for several weeks untouched by birds.

The gaultherias are a large genus with considerable variation in size and habit. In one or two the flowers are the main attraction, and even in those primarily grown for their fruit the flowers are large enough to make the shrubs attractive in late spring or early summer as well. The two most beautiful flowering shrubs are *G. sinensis* and *G. willisiana*, both ultimately growing to more than 1 ft (30 cm) high and having long sprays of white flowers in May, followed by insignificant fruits. Both are uncommon.

The best of the fruiting species are very worth while. Many of them seem to be quite slow-growing, and I plant them in choice spots in the peat bed, but they are generally easy enough for the front of the shrub border. In fact, *G. procumbens* is an exception in running underground and making a good vigorous ground-covering shrub, with white flowers and bright red berries. *G. cuneata* is much more choice, a neat compact shrub with very large white berries in autumn. *G. miqueliana* is usually a little taller and also has white or

113

pinkish fruits. Among the blue-berried species I like *G. trichophylla* best, a very neat plant up to 6 in (15 cm) high, with very beautiful turquoise fruits. *G. nummularioides* has even darker fruits on a low carpeting plant, which will spread quite widely in good peaty conditions.

Some vacciniums were mentioned in the early season section, but the best of all is as valuable as an autumn-fruiting plant as a spring-flowering plant. This is *Vaccinium vitis-idaea* 'Koralle', with abundant white flowers on a plant which I find takes several years to attain more than a foot high, but covers itself every autumn in big red berries which remain on the plant in good condition for several weeks.

One myrtle is worth mentioning, although it is quite uncommon. This is *Myrtus nummularia*, an absolutely prostrate mat of thin shoots with tiny leaves, which tend gradually to spread sideways, rooting at their nodes. The flowers are quite small, but they are followed by delightful large pink berries, which look as if they are sitting on the ground among the somewhat sparse stems.

4 Practical Matters

Construction

I wrote a few words about rock gardens, peat beds and raised beds in the first chapter, and I hope I shall be forgiven for saying very little more about the construction of rock gardens here. They are still being built by professionals – look at the spectacular examples at Chelsea each year – and they are being built by enthusiastic alpine growers. There are few garden features more beautiful than well-constructed rock gardens, built to fit in well with the landscape and thoughtfully planted. I am sure they will continue to be built, and detailed instructions for constructing 'natural rock gardens' can be found in specialised literature. However, I feel that the majority of gardeners wanting to use alpines creatively, especially in small gardens, would prefer the simpler method of making raised beds with low retaining-walls, or even to grow them on the flat.

Perhaps I should mention that some unbelievable eyesores are still being built in the name of rock gardens. Many years ago I witnessed a typical example of rock garden construction. Looking out at my neighbour's lawn one morning, I was surprised to see that a circular heap of top soil had been deposited upon it. By the end of the next day the heap was 'decorated' with pieces of Kentish ragstone, which had been dropped at intervals on to its surface. This particular type of construction was described some seventy years' ago as the 'almond pudding' by Reginald Farrer, not to be confused with the 'dog's graveyard', in which the stones are placed with their points, rather than their flat surfaces, inwards. Both of these look horrendous until the rocks have been completely hidden by robust plants, and have therefore become superfluous! Use rock by all means, but make it look like a natural outcrop or – much more simply – use it to make a series of raised beds, with the planting surfaces horizontal, so that the rain will not run off down a slope.

Over and over again I have mentioned the importance of good drainage and plenty of humus. It is very difficult to give precise advice about the grit to be used for drainage, as it depends on local sources. Here in Kent, we can easily obtain crushed 'beach', which is very sharp and which I use in a size of $\frac{3}{16}$th inch (0.6 cm) downwards – meaning everything that has passed through a $\frac{3}{16}$th inch (0.6 cm) sieve. In other areas, river sand, Cornish sand, or limestone chippings (not for acid beds!) may be more readily obtainable. Whatever the grit, it should be forked well into the top spit of soil in a quantity which depends on the heaviness of the soil as well as on the plants to be grown. For the more difficult alpines the mixture which I have described as 'rich scree' is ideal, with one half of its bulk grit and the other half a mixture of loam and peat. For most plants this can be reduced to one-third and two-thirds, but in heavy soils I would strongly recommend incorporating at least this amount of grit and preferably more. In the worst of stodgy clay, the best results are obtained with a minimum of work by covering the area with at least six inches of pure grit and planting directly into that. The plants will soon reach the nutrients beneath.

Humus generally has to mean peat, but leaf-mould is even better as it provides additional nutrients, bearing in mind that leaf-mould from alkaline woodland may not be acid, and may be unsuitable for gentians, Ericaceae, etc. For the general run of sun-loving plants, peat greatly improves moisture retention and I like to be generous with it, again forking it well into the top spit. For 'peat-bed' plants the final compost should be at least 50 per cent peat, with the remainder lime-free loam and grit in equal parts. Ideally, some of the peat should be replaced by leaf-mould.

In addition to incorporating grit into the soil, it is extremely helpful, when growing alpines together in a rock garden or raised bed, to surface the soil with half to one inch of pure grit. This stops small plants being battered by the rain, and has a dramatic effect in retaining moisture.

Peat-bed construction is very similar to raised-bed construction, except that peat blocks are classically used instead of walling stone. I say classically, because they are not always readily available, and very similar results can be obtained by using stones. Until recently all my own peat beds were of this construction, only differing from the other raised beds in the composition of the soil, which was two-thirds peat and leaf-mould and one-third grit, and maybe a little loam. Peat blocks look even better and, apart from their aesthetic value, the plants can actually root into them.

'Never use farmyard manure for alpines', books will tell you. Like most dogma I think this needs taking with a pinch of salt! Maybe if you are growing alpines only it is safe advice, although personally I use well-rotted manure at least 8 inches (20 cm) under the surface of beds where the many alpines liking rich but well-drained conditions are to be grown. Certainly keep it well away from the roots of newly planted alpines, and do not use it fresh. Throughout this book I have been recommending growing alpines with other plants, and this puts another complexion on the subject, because your other plants probably love manure! My own practice is to put plenty of manure at the bottom of each spit when first making a mixed border, and to avoid bringing it too near the surface. If I am going to grow alpines along the front, or even between shrubs, I fork in grit and peat, but I leave the manure eight inches down where I hope it will be appreciated by the alpines only when they are established. All my peat beds and other shady beds had the same treatment originally, but it must be remembered that most ericaceous shrubs are shallow-rooted and probably never reach the manure, which they dislike, whereas the deeper-rooting plants, which usually enjoy a rich soil, will find their way down to it.

Planting and Maintenance

I am a great believer in spring planting, although alpines are nearly always grown in containers and therefore can be planted at any time, unless the ground is frozen. In practice, most plants are bought on visits to shows, nurseries or garden centres, and are planted immediately. If you buy plants by mail order, they are most often sent in autumn or spring. Spring delivery is no problem, but I have found from long, and sometimes bitter experience that plants delivered in October or later, many of them dormant, suffer considerable losses if planted immediately. If you have a frame or cold greenhouse, it is much better to pot them up separately and keep them under glass until new growth begins in the spring. I even prefer to pot up dormant plants received in early spring until they acquire some top-growth – it is only too easy to plant something else too near a small dormant plant, however careful you are with labelling.

The one absolutely vital factor in successful planting is watering; this means continued watering until the plant is well established, and it may be necessary all through a dry summer! In recommending spring planting I am very aware that more watering will be necessary than in the autumn, but I remain unrepentant.

Nowadays most plants are grown commercially in peat-based composts, fed either with slow-relief fertiliser or with frequent liquid feeds. There are two important considerations here: the roots are going to suffer a dramatic change in compost when planted, and they may suffer from a shortage of nutrients if they are left in their original compost for a long time. I suggest you repot them or plant them quickly, knocking out the plants and loosening the roots as much as possible around the sides and bottom so that they come into immediate contact with the new soil – otherwise they may continue to go round and round the original compost until the plant dies of starvation. Some experienced growers even wash all the old soil off the roots before replanting, but I do not think this extreme root disturbance is necessary. When planting in the garden, unless a lot of peat has already been incorporated into the soil, I suggest that it helps the roots to adapt to their strange (unpeaty!) environment if you make the planting hole large enough to put a layer of peat, or preferably peat mixed with grit, in the gap between the old compost and the new. Make sure that the neck of the plant is at the same level after planting, especially with ericaceous plants, some of which hate being buried too deep, and then firm the ground around them and water thoroughly. If you have to plant in very dry soil the obvious advice is 'don't', but you can get excellent results by 'puddling them in'. This means that, after placing your plant in its hole and putting peat around it, you fill the hole with water two or three times, finally making sure it is filled to the right level with soil and firming gently. You can compact such wet soil too much.

Labelling is a major problem to anyone with a large collection of plants, especially if their owner's memory is diminishing! My own garden is labelled as completely as possible, and I accept the criticism that it looks like a cemetery, especially in winter! Visitors on the National Garden Scheme days are overjoyed to see the labels, photographers – myself included – are not! If you do not want to have visible labels I would recommend a plan of each bed, with the plants carefully marked on it for future reference as soon as they have been planted. If you do intend to label your plants, then you must face certain problems.

The most readily available and cheapest labels are white plastic – hence the cemetery appearance – and you have to find an indelible ink or pencil. The best ink I have found is fading fast after a year and may fade earlier. I find, somewhat unexpectedly, that soft pencil lasts better, but it shows up less easily. Aluminium labels marked with pencil last almost permanently, but are expensive. 'Dymo' tape on plastic fades and drops off after a year or two. I suspect that special indelible ink and an old-fashioned nib may be one possible answer for the patient gardener, but I find it very slow – a good job for those long winter evenings perhaps!

Propagation

Increasing plants is one of the most exciting branches of gardening. Vegetative propagation enables the gardener to have effective groups of a plant at minimum expense, and growing from seed can open up new realms, enabling the enthusiast to grow the remarkable range of plants from all over the world that are offered in the lists of special societies, as well as in commercial lists at home and abroad.

Vegetative Propagation

This generally means propagation by division or by cuttings. Division is perhaps the simplest method. Many of the larger herbaceous plants can be dug up, preferably in early spring, and pulled apart by hand or, in the case of large tough plants, by pushing two forks back to back into the clump and then levering the two portions apart. Large pieces can then be replanted immediately in prepared ground, so that one good plant purchased in spring can become a sizeable group after one year's growth. I hope nurserymen will forgive me! With smaller pieces of plant, which must have a few roots and at least one good growth bud, it is best to pot the pieces separately into a good compost such as John Innes No. 2, with at least one-third of its bulk of extra grit. At this stage I generally use a homemade compost of equal parts loam, peat and grit for the easy plants, with 50 per cent of grit for the trickier alpines. Keep the plants in a cold frame or cold house for a few weeks until they are growing well, and then plant them out.

The majority of plants can be propagated from cuttings. I have a small mist unit, which is excellent for anyone who wants to propagate in large quantities. It is labour-saving rather than miracle-working, the great advantage being that the cuttings can be left alone until they are rooted. Some plants, especially those with hairy leaves, dislike mist and root better by other methods, and in practice most, if not all plants, can be rooted without mist, although I think the accompanying bottom heat may be helpful.

Electric propagators with bottom heat and a plastic cover produce good quick results but are very expensive for the area they provide. The simplest method, which I recommend, is the use of trays ('propagators') fitted with a plastic cover, sometimes with ventilators in the roof, which are not essential. The rooting medium most often recommended is one of coarse sand with up to one-third of sieved peat added. After trying various methods, I have convinced myself that slightly better results are obtained by using Perlite instead of sand. I use the standard grade, obtainable from many garden centres, for larger cuttings, and the fine 'seed grade' for smaller cuttings. The trays are filled to the rim with the chosen medium, which is then pressed down gently and watered well with a fine rose. It is then ready to receive the cuttings.

Cuttings are best taken in cool conditions and must not be allowed to wilt. On a warm day, work in the shade, keep spraying them with water and, if you cannot deal with them immediately, keep them in a plastic bag. The cuttings are taken with a very sharp knife or razor blade making a sloping cut just below a node – the point at which a leaf or shoot comes out of the stem. Remove any leaves from the bottom of the cutting (i.e. leaves which would be buried when the cutting is planted), preferably by cutting them off cleanly, although, against all the rules, I usually pull them off, unless I notice that this tears the bark. As deliberate wounding of difficult cuttings is often advocated, I am not convinced that the damage of tearing matters! Ideally, the cuttings should be inserted so that they are not quite touching. Dipping the cutting in rooting hormone is probably worth while. I use a liquid (almost a jelly) preparation, which also contains the fungicide Captan, and I am reasonably happy with results.

The cuttings must never be allowed to dry out, but with a well-fitting plastic cover they will only need an occasional watering with a fine spray. When some new growth is apparent try pulling a cutting gently. If it comes out or you feel small roots breaking you are being premature and should put it back and leave the rest of the cuttings until they are firmly rooted. They can then be potted separately into the sort of compost I have already advocated for divisions.

Another method often recommended is to put the cuttings into pots and place them in polythene bags fastened with a closure, or put upturned bags over them. Some care is needed not to have the compost too wet initially if you use this method for woolly-leaved plants.

Seed

Growing plants from seed never ceases to excite me – in fact, I sow a ridiculous number of seeds every year, from my own plants, from friends' plants, from the seed lists of specialist societies at home and abroad, and from overseas collecting expeditions which occasionally advertise for subscribers.

Raising alpine plants is extremely simple because, far from requiring any heat, your pots after sowing should be kept as cold as possible. Experts differ in their choice of composts. John Innes Seed Compost was the favourite for many years and still gives good results. Peat-based seed composts have become increasingly popular and are ideal for plants which like moist or acid conditions, although for the latter they must be lime-free or 'ericaceous' composts. For alpines I would always add plenty of extra coarse sand or fine Perlite to the bought compost – they never seem to me to have enough drainage. My own pet compost of the moment is made up of equal parts of sterile loam, sieved moss peat and seed-grade Perlite, with Superphosphate at the rate of $1\frac{1}{2}$ oz (43 gm) to 8 gallons (36 litres), and lime $\frac{3}{4}$ oz (21 gm) to 8 gallons (36 litres), except for lime-haters. These are the quantities of fertiliser in John Innes Seed Compost. I prefer plastic pots for seed-sowing as they dry out more slowly, and I use square ones to take up less space, the size of pot depending on the quantity of seed available. 'Sow thinly' is the classic advice, which can be modified with experience, when you discover that certain seed nearly always germinates badly and you can afford to sow it thickly. Celmisias are a typical example. The ideal to aim at is to have seedlings nearly, but not quite, touching at pricking-out stage – a policy of perfection, especially as I would conversely advise pricking out if they do touch!

When filling the pots with your chosen compost, leave a space after firming of about half an inch for covering and to ensure adequate watering. Sow the seed 'thinly' and cover by sieving enough compost on the surface just to hide the seed. With fat seeds it will not matter if you use $\frac{1}{4}$ in (0.5 cm), but for fine seed use little or none, because you are then going to cover the surface with $\frac{1}{4}$ in (0.5 cm) of small clean grit. I use the smallest available flint grit, sold as 'chick grit' in different sizes, but aquarium gravel and other materials will work as well. The main object is that you should be able to water the seed pans from overhead without disturbing the seed beneath, and also to help retain moisture.

After sowing and watering, keep the pots outside in a shady place where you can reach them easily with water, and where they will be frozen and rained upon during winter.

The time of sowing is of some importance, but a lot depends on when your seed is available. Very often this is not until the autumn or winter, sometimes even late winter, and I would then always recommend sowing it immediately to get the benefit of any cold weather, which helps germination in most alpines. If you have your own or other seed available earlier, then the best treatment depends on whether you have a greenhouse or frame available. There is a lot to be said in favour of sowing immediately the seed is ripe, in fact it may be essential for certain families and genera, for example corydalis, and many of the Primulaceae and Compositae. 'When in doubt sow immediately' is good advice, but problems arise on those occasions when the seed germinates quickly – early sowing may not mean early germination! The young seedlings appearing early will probably need special care and attention during their first winter – hence the need for glass protection. If you have no glass, it may be better to keep seed, unless it can be sown before August, until the cold weather comes, and you will know there is unlikely to be any germination until spring.

As I write we are enjoying an exceptionally mild winter and many seedlings are appearing in December, just to confound me!

Once germination occurs you can bring the seed pan into more light, although it will need some shading in a greenhouse or frame in summer. The best time to prick out the seedlings is usually said to be when they have formed their first true leaves and this is a good general principle. Occasionally you will have pans which have been sown too thickly – I certainly do – and the seedlings are then in great danger of dying, usually rapidly and totally, from fungus infection. It is then advisable to prick out at least a proportion while they are still at the cotyledon (seed-leaf) stage. When you feel the seedlings are ready, knock out the contents of the pot and gently separate them without damaging their roots. I find this is much easier when Perlite has been used to give the extra drainage. The seedlings can then be potted separately, or, if they are very small, several to a pot or tray. The compost can be John Innes No. 1 with extra grit, or a compost with Perlite similar to that recommended for seed-sowing but with John Innes Base instead of Superphosphate, in the strength for John Innes No. 1 ($\frac{1}{2}$ oz to 1 gallon, or 14 gm to 4.5 litres).

The young potted seedlings are then kept watered, with some shading, until they are large enough to plant into the garden or to repot into larger pots, with John Innes No. 2 compost or its equivalent.

Growing bulbs from seed is just as easy but requires a little more patience, as you will have to wait probably from three to five years. That sounds a long time, but if you keep sowing some every year you will soon forget the passage of time, with good stocks of new and exciting bulbs coming into flower every year. The main difference in treatment is that I would sow into John Innes No. 1, or its equivalent Perlite mixture, and I would keep the seedlings in the original pots for two growing seasons. Then knock out the contents towards the end of their dormant period, say in August, and find the young bulbs – very exciting – which will usually be near or even on the bottom of the pot. They will probably still be rather small for the garden, and should be repotted into John Innes No. 2 for another year or two before planting out.

Plants for Special Situations

Walls

In the course of the previous descriptions I have drawn attention to many plants which grow well planted on their sides, and this makes them ideal wall plants. In addition to these, there are plants which look their best tumbling over the edge of a wall and down its face, and finally plants which grow along the interstices of the rocks, filling them with their growth.

Sunny Walls

I suggested earlier that sunny walls are far and away the most satisfactory sites for planting the most vigorous ground-covering plants, such as aubretia, arabis and the larger alyssums. These can be planted in spaces in the rockwork as well as on the edge, so that the whole wall becomes a mass of colour in the spring. The more vigorous varieties of *Phlox subulata* and *P. douglasii* can be used in the same way and can be followed later by other carpeters such as *Genista procumbens* (which is one of the comparatively few plants that will grow downwards) and *Convolvulus sabatius*, in a sunny and sheltered position.

Apart from these plants, which will follow the contours of the rock face, there are many others which you can plant in spaces between the rocks, especially those which are usually found in rock crevices in their natural habitat. If you have suitable small plants available, I strongly recommend planting them as you construct the wall. Have some good gritty compost to hand and put a layer of it on top of each course of rocks. Then lay the plants on the compost and cover the roots over completely with it before putting a further rock course on top of them. This may be a policy of perfection, but it is much easier than the alternative of gouging out holes and cracks in an established retaining wall.

Some of my favourite alpines to plant on their sides in walls are the larger lewisias, preferably in some shade in the south, the silver-encrusted saxifrages, *Primula marginata* and *Verbascum dumulosum*; all have rosettes which will protrude from the wall surface. Other plants can be used to fill up the actual crevices of the wall without protruding far: for example, the smaller-rosetted saxifrages such as the *S. aizoon* varieties, or the more vigorous kabschias, any of the innumerable sempervivums and the smaller creeping campanulas. As long as the soil behind the wall has been well prepared it is worth trying almost any alpines of suitable low-growing habit, of which you have spare plants. If you have to plant into an established wall, use the youngest plants possible – they will settle down much better than those with a fat rootball that may have to be squashed into a small hole.

Shady Walls

Even in deep shade it is possible to find plants to brighten a retaining wall. Again I would stress the importance of good soil for the plants to root into. I have mentioned the possible use of lewisias, especially in the south where sunny walls seem to be too hot for them, but the classic plants for this situation are the ramondas and haberleas, which, when planted on their sides, revel in a shady place where they cannot suffer from too much water sitting among their rosettes. More unorthodox, but I find effective, are the smaller heucheras and also many of the shade-loving saxifrages, the 'mossies' and the small 'London Prides', for example, which will fill in cracks in the same way as their sun-loving relations.

Among the carpeting plants for shade there is less scope, but the varieties of *Phlox adsurgens* and the varieties of *P. stolonifera* and *P. procumbens* are well worth trying along the top of shady walls, although you may find that some of them object to growing downwards!

Plants for Dry Shade

This is a difficult situation, as I discussed earlier, and the vital question is 'how dry?' Everything possible must be done to incorporate humus, and if this is successful then any of the more vigorous shade-lovers can be grown.

Some of the most exciting plants worth trying in these conditions are undoubtedly the cyclamen, especially *C. hederifolium* and *C. coum*. I am amazed how well they have done in a dry border in my garden, even when very close to a box hedge, but the bed was well dug originally. Cyclamen perhaps are the elite, and in very dry conditions you are dependent on such really easy plants as the hardy geraniums – probably your best choice – or even such excessively vigorous plants as the forms of *Vinca major* and *Vinca minor*. *Viola labradorica* I find will grow anywhere; in fact, I cannot get rid of it once it has begun to seed around.

The easier lamiums such as 'White Nancy' and 'Chequers' come into the same category. I find them extremely easy and they will put up with dry conditions without getting as out of hand as the periwinkles. With a little more humus and moisture you should be able to grow pulmonarias, their vigour depending very much on the quality of soil preparation. The same applies to the epimediums and vancouverias, the more robust of which can become too vigorous in good conditions but will cope adequately with moderately dry shade. In describing the dicentras I also suggested some which would put up with similar conditions, especially *D. formosa* and the more vigorous spreaders.

Plants for Wet Conditions

Although moist shade is an ideal situation for many wonderful woodland plants, wet conditions combined with a heavy poorly-drained soil are anathema to most alpines, and the first priority is to attempt to improve the situation by digging in plenty of drainage material and humus.

When discussing shade-loving alpines I referred to several plants that enjoy wet conditions, but to very few which will put up with bad drainage. Among the primulas, so important for any moist situation, there are one or two which will thrive in sticky conditions, notably *Primula rosea*, *P. florindae* and *P. sikkimensis*, but others of the Candelabra section are always worth trying. In other genera the choice is limited, but some of the dwarf astilbes and mimulus will enjoy the same conditions, growing among the larger perennial bog plants including the *sibirica* irises, lysichitons, calthas and others. One of the great problems of bog gardening is that the plants which do well sometimes do excessively well, and if you are trying to grow some of the daintier plants care must be taken not to let them become overwhelmed by the 'thugs'.

Alpines Requiring Protection

Throughout the book I have made occasional mention of plants which need specialised conditions, which are more easily provided in an alpine house or cold frame. Detailed growing methods under glass do not come within the scope of this book, but anyone who grows a range of easier alpines will sooner or later want to try the more difficult ones. For comprehensive instruction I would refer them to specialist literature describing all aspects of growing under glass.

Many gardeners lack these facilities or prefer to grow all their plants in the open, and, as I have suggested throughout the book, there are comparatively few plants for which protection is essential if they are given excellent drainage. One compromise which I have used successfully in my own garden is to grow these plants in a raised bed built to accommodate a frame over it in winter, perhaps from late October to March. A simpler method which may enable tricky plants to survive the winter outside is to prop panes of glass or cloches over their heads. The obvious disadvantage is that if done on a large scale it can be unsightly.

Troughs and other Containers

In these days of small gardens and patios the use of containers is enjoying an increasing vogue, and there is no reason why any sort of container should not be used for alpines. Old stone troughs are, of course, the ideal setting and they look beautiful planted with suitable alpines, with a careful eye to scale. Unfortunately, they have become rare and expensive, but similar quite pleasing troughs can be made from a mixture that has been called 'hypertufa', consisting of peat 2 parts, cement 1 part and sand 1 part. Glazed sinks are hideous, but they can be greatly improved by covering with a layer of hypertufa, having first painted the glazed surface with an adhesive such as Unibond.

The compost used in containers can be varied for different plant combinations, but bear in mind that they dry out quickly, so it is as well to use plenty of humus and rather less grit than suggested for pots. John Innes No. 3 with extra grit and one-third of its bulk of humus would be suitable.

Planting of containers needs careful thought, as it is easy to make mistakes. I have one trough that was planted originally with kabschia saxifrages, with a 'dwarf' *Taxus* and with the beautiful compact *Daphne arbuscula*. Now the *Taxus* has swamped all the saxifrages and half the *Daphne*, which in turn has spoilt the shape of the conifer. Something should have gone long ago and it is now too late, without replanting the whole trough! One moral of this tale is to be very careful of so-called 'dwarf' conifers. The only ones likely to be suitable are the beautiful upright-growing *Juniperus communis* var. *compressa*, or the tightest possible buns among the forms of *Chamaecyparis obtusa*. *Daphne arbuscula* is probably the largest species suitable for any normal-sized trough, but even so you must be prepared to move plants from around it as the years go by.

I am not going to suggest specific plants for containers, as any small alpines are suitable and I have already drawn attention to some of the best. If you are combining small alpines with bulbs it is important to consider the scale of the bulbs and only use the smallest-growing species, for example *Narcissus asturiensis*, any cyclamen, the smaller corydalis, most of the species crocus and a few of the smallest fritillaries.

Although space is limited, I think containers look best with some rock in them, preferably tufa, which will eventually become colonised with seedlings or with plants spreading over the surface, to become an integral part of the container.

Tufa

This is a remarkable medium for growing alpines, especially the difficult ones – it is a very soft light rock, which can be obtained from specialist nurseries in any size, from a few inches square to a massive boulder. I use it as the rock in troughs and raised beds, but there is no reason why it cannot be used as the basic material for large rock gardens. One famous alpine garden has a tufa cliff about 7 ft (2.1 m) high and several yards long, planted with an astonishing collection of plants which are generally considered difficult to grow in the open.

The great joy of tufa is that it is so soft that planting holes can easily be made in it with an old chisel or screwdriver. Ideally, the hole should be about an inch across and deep enough to accommodate all the roots of a young plant comfortably, filling the space around them with gritty compost. Young seedlings are ideal, although larger holes can be made to take more established plants. Several plants suitable for tufa have been mentioned, but most high alpines and cushion plants, unless they are lime-haters, will flourish in it, and there is endless scope for experiment.

Pests and Diseases

For the gardener wanting to grow a collection of alpines in the open pests and diseases present few problems, no more than with herbaceous plants and certainly less than with roses. I feel justified in making light of them and keeping this section short!

Among pests, slugs are usually the worst and must be dealt with if necessary by the usual pellets or liquid slug-killers (but don't forget that these can harm children and domestic animals). Mice and birds can both be troublesome, especially if you grow many bulbs. Cats or traps can help with the former, and cottoning with the latter. It may be necessary to prevent entry of birds into frames or houses with netting, as birds can be very destructive to cushion plants, pulling them to pieces, apparently for amusement!

Apart from the larger pests, aphis, white fly and red spider can attack alpines, but they are rarely a problem except under glass and they can be treated effectively with modern insecticides.

Fungus diseases may also be an occasional problem, again mainly under glass and again mainly treatable with modern fungicides. Viruses are the most serious scourge of modern gardens, but in practice they rarely seem to affect alpine plants, although I have seen them in irises, primulas and lewisias. If you think you have an infected plant it is probably advisable to seek expert advice, as the plant should unquestionably be destroyed if it is infected.

Further Reading

The Alpine Garden Society has produced many authoritative books on alpine plants, including *Alpine Gardening: A Beginner's Guide*, *Handbook of Rock Gardening* and *Alpines in Pots*. There are also their books on specific genera including Cyclamen, Saxifrages, Primulas, Hellebores, and several others.

Other books which can be recommended are *Alpines for your Garden* by Alan Bloom (Floraprint, 1980), *Collins Guide to Alpines and Rock Garden Plants* by Anna Griffith (Collins, 1985), and *Manual of Alpine Plants* (Hamlyn, 1986) by Ingwersen. Christopher Helm together in the USA with Timber Press has now embarked on a most useful Rock Gardener's Library of which this volume forms a part. Other titles in this series are: *A Manual of Alpine and Rock Garden Plants* edited by Christopher Grey-Wilson; *A Guide to Rock Gardening* by Richard Bird; and *The Alpine House* by Robert Rolfe. Two other important monographs on specific genera should be mentioned; *The Genus Lewisia*, a Kew Magazine Monograph by Brian Mathew (Helm and Timber Press, 1989) and *Saxifrages of Europe* by David Webb and Richard Gornall (Helm and Timber Press, 1989).

Specialist Societies

The Alpine Garden Society
The Scottish Rock Garden Club

These two societies are invaluable to anyone with an interest in alpine plants. They regularly produce excellent bulletins as well as very comprehensive seed lists, and arrange shows and meetings around the country.

For anyone interested in the flowers of the United States or New Zealand, the American Rock Garden Society and the New Zealand Alpine Garden Society also send regular bulletins and seed lists to overseas members.

Alpine Garden Society, Lye End Link, St Johns, Woking, Surrey GU21 1SW

Scottish Rock Garden Club, 21 Merchiston Park, Edinburgh EH10 4PW

American Rock Garden Society, 15 Fairmead Rd, Darien, Connecticut 06820, USA

New Zealand Alpine Garden Society, 238 Greers Rd, Christchurch 5, New Zealand.

Appendix
Sun-loving Alpines and Shade-loving Alpines

KEY TO TABLES

Colour	Relates to flowers, unless the plant is grown mainly for its foliage.
Height and Spread	Very approximate measurements (in cm), after two or three years' growth.
Season	Month of flowering. Very variable, depending on geographical location.
Soil	OS = Ordinary soil, with reasonable drainage.
	RS = Rich scree, i.e. with plenty of peat or leaf-mould and one-third to one-half of its bulk as grit.
	Scree = as for RS, but with at least half of its bulk as grit.
	W = Woodland, with half of its bulk as peat or leaf-mould.
	AH = Alpine House or Cold Greenhouse.

TABLE 1   Sun-loving alpines

Name	Colour	Height (cm)	Spread (cm)	Season	Soil	Special features
Achillea tomentosa	Yellow	15–20	30–50	5–6	OS	Runs gently
Aciphylla pinnatifida	Bronze leaves	15–20	15–20	All	RS	Dangerously spiky rosettes
Aciphylla (other species)	Bronze leaves	10–100	10–100	All	RS	Dangerously spiky rosettes
Adonis amurensis	Yellow	20–40	15–25	3–4	OS	Good foliage
Adonis vernalis	Yellow	15–20	15–25	3–4	OS	Good foliage
Aethionema grandiflora	Pink	15–25	20–30	5–6	OS	Shrubby
Aethionema 'Warley Rose'	Pink	15–25	20–30	5–6	OS	Shrubby
Alchemilla alpina	Green	10–15	25–30	5–6	OS	Good foliage
Alchemilla erythropoda	Green	10–15	25–30	5–6	OS	Good foliage
Anacyclus depressus	White, red reverse	3–5	25–50	5–6	Scree or AH	
Anagallis tenella 'Studland'	Pink	2–4	25–30	5–6	RS	Low carpeter
Anchusa caespitosa	Blue	3–5	20–30	5–6	Scree or AH	
Andryala agardhii	Yellow	18–30	20–30	6–7	RS	Silver leaves

TABLE 1 *Continued*

Name	Colour	Height (cm)	Spread (cm)	Season	Soil	Special features
Anthyllis hermanniae	Yellow	30–60	40–80	6–7	OS	Compact shrub
Armeria caespitosa	Pink	8–16	15–30	4–5	RS	The best thrift
Arnebia echioides	Yellow, brown spots	30–40	30–40	6–7	OS	The 'Prophet flower'
Artemisia pedemontana	Silver leaves	10–16	30–60	All	OS	
Artemisia stelleriana	Silver leaves	10–16	50–100	4–11	OS	
Arthropodium candidum	White	15–25	20–40	6–7	OS	Dainty sprays of flowers
Arthropodium milleflorum	Pale violet	30–60	15–30	6–7	OS	Dainty sprays of flowers
Asperula nitida (*A. puberula*)	Pink	6–10	20–30	4–5	RS	Good cushion
Asperula suberosa	Pink	6–10	10–20	4–5	Scree	Excellent for AH
Asphodelus acaulis	Pink	12–20	15–30	2–3	Scree or AH	
Brachycome rigida	Blue	10–15	12–20	6–7	RS	
Carlina acaulis	Off-white	10–20	20–30	6–7	OS	Stemless thistle
Celsia acaulis (*Verbascum acaule*)	Yellow	5–10	10–20	5–6	RS	Miniature verbascum
Celsioverbascum 'Golden Wings'	Yellow	20–30	20–30	5–6	RS	
Centaurea bella	Mauve	15–20	30–60	6–7	OS	Silver leaves
Centaurea pulchra	Mauve	15–20	50–100	6–7	OS	Can spread!
Chrysanthemum weyrichii	Pink	15–20	30–50	8–10	OS	
Clematis marmoraria	White	10–20	10–20	4–5	RS	Small shrub
Corethrogyne californica	Pale mauve	20–30	20–40	7–8	RS	Silver leaves
Coronilla minima	Yellow	10–15	25–60	5–6	RS	Runs underground
Crassula sarcocaulis	Pink	20–30	20–30	9–10	OS	Neat shrub
Crepis incana	Pink	20–30	20–30	7–8	OS	Good wall plant

129

TABLE 1 *Continued*

Name	Colour	Height (cm)	Spread (cm)	Season	Soil	Special features
Deutzia 'Nikko'	White	30–40	30–40	5–6	OS	Shrub
Diosphaera asperuloides (*Trachelium asperuloides*)	Blue	3–5	12–20	5–6	Scree or AH	Cushion plant
Diplarrhena moraea 'Nana'	White	15–20	10–15	6–7	OS	Iris-like
Dracocephalum argunense	Blue	25–30	20–25	7–8	OS	
Dryas octopetala	White	5–10	30–60	4–5	OS	Carpeter
Epilobium kai-koense	Pink	8–12	8–12	6–7	OS	No excessive seeding
Erigeron aureus	Deep yellow	10–15	12–18	5–6	RS	
Erigeron 'Canary Bird'	Pale yellow	10–15	12–18	5–6	RS	
Erinacea anthyllis	Blue	15–25	20–30	5–6	RS	Compact spiny shrub
Erinus alpinus	Pink or white	10–15	8–12	5–7	OS	Seeds freely
Euryops acraeus	Yellow	20–30	20–30	5–7	RS	Fine silver leaves
Geum montanum	Yellow	15–20	25–40	4–5	OS	
Globularia bellidifolia	Blue	8–12	15–30	5–6	RS	
Globularia trichosantha	Blue	10–15	15–30	5–6	RS	
Haplopappus coronopifolius	Yellow	20–30	25–35	7–8	OS	
Inula ensifolia	Yellow	15–25	20–30	8–9	OS	
Jasminum parkeri	Yellow	15–30	15–30	5–6	OS	Neat shrub
Leontopodium alpinum	White	15–25	10–20	4–5	RS	Edelweiss
Linanthastrum nuttallii	White	15–20	15–25	6–7	RS	Ferny leaves
Linaria alpina	Pink and blue	8–12	8–12	4–5	RS	Short-lived but seeds freely
Linaria tristis 'Toubkal'	Grey	8–12	8–12	5–6	RS	Glaucous leaves
Matthiola fruticulosa valesiaca	Pink	10–15	20–40	5–7	RS	Runs underground – not excessively
Morisia monanthos	Yellow	5–8	8–12	4–5	RS	Neat rosettes
Nierembergia rivularis	White	5–10	30–50	6–7	OS	Spreading carpeter

TABLE 1 *Continued*

Name	Colour	Height (cm)	Spread (cm)	Season	Soil	Special features
Omphalodes luciliae	Blue	8–15	8–15	5–6	RS or AH	Glaucous leaves
Onosma albo-roseum	White to pink	25–35	30–50	6–7	RS	Excellent wall plant
Onosma tauricum	Yellow	25–35	30–50	6–7	RS	Excellent wall plant
Parochetus communis	Blue	5–10	20–30	7–9	OS	Slightly tender
Phuopsis stylosa	Pink	10–15	30–50	6–8	OS	Easy carpeter
Physoplexis comosa (Phyteuma comosa)	Pale lavender	10–15	10–15	5–6	Scree or AH	Unusual alpine house plant
Platycodon apoyama	Blue	30–50	30–50	7–8	OS	Large flowers
Pleurospermum brunonis	White	15–20	15–30	7–8	OS	Excellent Umbellifer
Polemonium confertum	Blue	20–25	15–30	5–6	RS	
Polemonium brandegeei	Yellow	20–25	20–30	6–7	RS	
Potentilla nitida	Pink	5–10	10–20	4–5	Scree	Silver leaves
Potentilla tonguei	Peach	12–18	20–40	5–6	OS	
Ptilotrichum spinosum	Pink	20–30	20–30	5–6	OS	Silver shrub
Raoulia australis	Silver leaves	1	20–40	All	RS	Flat carpet
Raoulia tenuicaulis	Silvery green	1	20–40	All	RS	Flat carpet
Saponaria × olivana	Deep pink	8–12	12–20	5–6	RS	Good cushion
Scabiosa 'Butterfly Blue'	Blue	30–40	25–35	5–10	OS	Long season
Silene hookeri	Pink	8–15	10–15	5–6	Scree or AH	Good AH plant
Tanacetum densum amani	Silver	12–15	20–30	All	RS	Silver foliage
Teucrium aroanum	Purple	4–8	10–20	6–7	RS	Grey leaves
Trollius acaulis	Yellow	6–10	10–15	4–5	OS	Damp-lover
Tunica saxifraga	Pink	12–18	20–30	7–8	OS	

131

TABLE 1 *Continued*

Name	Colour	Height (cm)	Spread (cm)	Season	Soil	Special features
Verbena chamaedrifolia (*V. peruviana*)	Red	5–10	20–30	6–9	OS	Tender
Veronica austraica (*V. teucrium*)	Blue	15–30	20–40	6–8	OS	Various cultivars
Veronica bombycina	Blue	4–6	10–15	5–6	Scree	White leaves
Veronica gentianoides	Blue	30–40	20–30	6–7	OS	Good variegated form
Veronica prostrata (*V. rupestris*)	Blue	20–30	20–40	6–7	OS	Various cultivars
Veronica spicata incana	Blue	20–30	20–30	6–7	OS	Silver leaves

TABLE 2 *Shade-loving alpines*

Name	Colour	Height (cm)	Spread (cm)	Season	Soil	Special features
Anemonella thalictroides	Pink or white	10–15	10–15	4–5	W	
Anemonopsis macrophylla	Purple	40–60	30–50	5–6	W	
Asarum europaeum	Brown	10–15	20–30	5–6	W or OS	Good glossy dark leaves
Caltha introloba	Pale pink	4–6	5–10	3–4	W	Very small
Deinanthe coerulea	Blue	15–30	20–30	5–6	W	
Gunnera prorepens	Red fruits	10–15	20–30	6–8	OS or W	Low creeper
Heloniopsis japonica	Pink	20–30	20–30	4–5	OS or W	
Jovellana sinclairii	White with blue spots	10–15	20–30	5–6	OS or W	Slightly tender
Linnaea borealis	Pink	5–10	30–40	4–5	W	
Liriope muscari	Blue	30–40	20–30	8–9	OS	Muscari-like flowers
Lithophragma parviflora	Pink	15–20	20–30	4–5	OS or W	
Omphalodes cappadocica	Blue	30–40	30–40	3–4	OS or W	
Omphalogramma vincaeflora	Violet	10–15	10–20	3–5	RS or W	Difficult in southern England
Paris polyphylla	Green	50–80	30–50	6–9	W	Green flowers and orange fruits
Patrinia triloba	Yellow	20–30	20–30	6–7	OS or W	
Philesia magellanica	Crimson	20–30	20–40	5–6	W	Spectacular but temperamental
Romanzoffia unalaschkensis	White	12–20	15–30	5–6	W	Good dark green leaves
Wulfenia carinthiaca	Blue	20–30	20–30	5–6	OS	Good crevice plant

Index

137